CHAIR YOGA FOR SENIORS

50, 60 and Beyond

Gentle Chair Yoga and Stretches to improve Flexibility, Balance and Relieve Aches and Pain.
Fully illustrated + Free Audiobook

DAVID O'CONNOR
FLORENCE GAUTHIER

Winner of the Senior Topics Firebird Book Award 2024

SECOND EDITION

© Copyright 2024 - All rights reserved.

The content contained within this book may not be reproduced, duplicated or transmitted without direct written permission from the author or the publisher.

Under no circumstances will any blame or legal responsibility be held against the publisher, or author, for any damages, reparation, or monetary loss due to the information contained within this book, either directly or indirectly.

Legal Notice:

This book is copyright protected. It is only for personal use. You cannot amend, distribute, sell, use, quote or paraphrase any part, or the content within this book, without the consent of the author or publisher.

Disclaimer Notice:

Please note the information contained within this document is for educational and entertainment purposes only. All effort has been executed to present accurate, up to date, reliable, complete information. No warranties of any kind are declared or implied. Readers acknowledge that the author is not engaged in the rendering of legal, financial, medical or professional advice. The content within this book has been derived from various sources. Please consult a licensed professional before attempting any techniques outlined in this book.

By reading this document, the reader agrees that under no circumstances is the author responsible for any losses, direct or indirect, that are incurred as a result of the use of the information contained within this document, including, but not limited to, errors, omissions, or inaccuracies.

TABLE OF CONTENTS

DEDICATION

This book is dedicated to all the brave hearts with decades of life experience, of enduring wear and tear, of triumphs and tribulations, and now looking to live a further purposeful life. It is comforting to realize that we do not encounter many golden-agers who long to be younger again. It appears from conversations that one would not trade the peaceful wisdom of old age for anything. Like everything else aging comes with, along with its challenges, rest assured that the practice of chair yoga will give wings to your creativity and resilience.

FOREWORD

How Chair Yoga Promotes Weight Loss

I received an email from Jim (Kanas City) who asked why *Chair Yoga for Seniors 50, 60 and Beyond* doesn't provide a 21 or 28 day weight loss plan like many chair yoga books for seniors.

A quick search on Amazon showed that many chair yoga books have prominent claims on their cover such as '21 day weight loss challenge', 'Chair Yoga for Rapid Weight Loss', 'Fat Burn 28 day challenge' and the like.

Jim's email deserved a detailed reply. I thought it important to clear any misunderstandings about the benefits chair yoga can offer with regard to weight loss and also how those benefits are achieved.

How Do You Lose Weight?

There are several factors involved in weight loss such as, metabolism, age, daily activity level, and current weight but basically losing weight comes down to a simple equation. You need to burn more calories than you consume, creating an energy (calorie) deficit.

To lose a pound of fat you must **burn approximately 3,500 calories** more than you consume. Or to put it another way, to lose one pound in a week, you need to burn 500 calories more than you consume each day.

But that is not as easy as it sounds. In fact relying purely on exercise (any exercise) creating this calorie deficit is very hard!

By way of an example:

- A **Krispy Kreme** glazed doughnut contains 340 calories,
- A **double chocolate doughnut** (my favorite) a whopping 400 calories
- **3 KFC** original recipe chicken wings 525 calories

According to a study by the U.S. Department of Health and Human Services, you burn between *120 to 250 calories with a 30-minute chair exercise routine*. This equates to approximately 4 to 8.3 calories per minute of chair yoga.

Many book covers shout '*lose weight rapidly with only 10 minutes a day of gentle chair yoga.*' But is that realistic? Do the maths, 10 minutes x 8.3 calories = *83 calories burned per chair yoga workout*, which is significantly short of the 500 per day calorie deficit required to lose just one pound of weight in a week.

You would need to perform chair yoga for **40 minutes** to burn off just one glazed doughnut!

Does Chair Yoga Promote Weight Loss?

Most Definitely YES!!

OK, we've established that '*calorie burn*' is not the main way chair yoga helps with weight loss, instead it supports the weight loss journey in other ways and fosters a healthier lifestyle.

- Chair yoga gradually improves overall flexibility and mobility making daily activities easier and reducing the risk of injury. You'll be able to do more, walk further, exercise for longer which imperceptibly increases the calories you naturally burn each day.

- Chair yoga teaches breathing techniques and clearing one's mind of negative thoughts. Studies have shown that these techniques help reduce stress, anxiety and depression by suppressing the production of the stress hormone Cortisol, which is linked to weight gain.
- Feeling less stressed also assists with other aspects of losing weight such as forming healthy eating habits. When you're stressed it's far too easy to reach for the chocolate or another slice of cake. I'm sure we have all been guilty of 'comfort' eating when our stress levels are high.
- Chair yoga is so much more than a collection of poses intended to build strength, it's the harmonization of body, mind and spirit. You achieve a greater introspection, awareness of your body, your emotions and its needs, often referred to as Mindfulness. Greater awareness fosters healthy habits reducing the likelihood of overeating, late-night snacking and binge eating.
- As we age our metabolism, the process by which our bodies convert food into energy, tends to slow making it harder to maintain a healthy weight. Chair yoga increases the blood flow throughout the body, including to the stomach stimulating the digestive system helping it to counteract this age related slowing of the metabolism by promoting better nutrient absorption.
- While chair yoga poses targeting specific areas such as core, arms, legs and back may be gentle and are performed slowly they still strengthen and build muscle mass. More muscle has several benefits, improved posture, better balance and greater strength, attributes which are advantageous at any age but particularly useful to combat the aging process. Muscles also *burn more calories*, even when you're at rest, than body fat.

To achieve these benefits it is therefore **vital that a chair yoga book be more than a collection of simple bullet point pose instructions.** What elevates chair yoga beyond mere callisthenics, to harness it's weight loss potential, is the harmonization of body, mind and spirit. Therefore, to access the many non-physical benefits an understanding of yoga principles, rather than simply knowing how to correctly position one's body, is necessary. If you notice that my pose instructions occasionally become a little talk-heavy, please appreciate that it is not to be bothersome; rather, it is to inform and remind you of the 'traditional yoga' intentions behind each move. It is actually the emphasis on holistic health, rather than the calorie burn, that enables chair yoga to play such an important role in a healthy weight loss program. That is also why I advocate popping on the headphones and with eyes closed following the audio instructions. As the audio creates the 'peaceful feel' of being in a yoga class listening to the voice of a teacher (yogi) you may find it easier to clear your mind, letting go of the day's frustrations, and to focus on your breath to promote relaxation and stress reduction.

In summary, Chair yoga is not an intensive form of activity, quite the opposite it should be performed slowly. It burns less calories than more strenuous activities and other forms of exercise therefore, calorie burn is not one of the main ways chair yoga assists with weight loss.

However, chair yoga is **perfect for seniors seeking to lose weight** being a form of exercise that is accessible to all. Chair yoga's role in weight loss is achieved by addressing mental and emotional barriers and by promoting healthy habits which support long-term sustainable weight loss and a healthier lifestyle as we age.

Consistency is the key! Remember to listen to your body, be patient and kind to yourself and progress at a pace that feels right for you.

Don't expect to lose weight in 21 days by only performing gentle chair yoga for a few minutes a day, **that simply isn't feasible.**

Avoid - '*Snake Oil Sellers*' who say you can *rapidly lose weight* with gentle chair yoga!

- If you make a habit of fitting *10 minutes chair yoga into your daily schedule and combine that with a healthy balanced diet* you will gradually shed the pounds, leading to sustainable weight loss and a healthier lifestyle!

Accept - that it takes time to lose weight and avoid fad diets, the latest crash diet seldom leads to lasting weight loss.

- The old adage, **'***Rome wasn't built in a day***'** holds true for healthy weight loss! You are also more likely to keep the weight off avoiding the 'yo-yo' effect many experience when attempting to rapidly lose weight.

Appreciate - the many wonderful benefits Chair Yoga provides seniors that enhance their life:

- Improved flexibility and mobility
- Increased muscle strength

- Better balance and coordination
- Stress and pain management
- Quality sleep
- Boosts confidence and reduces depression and anxiety
- Sense of Wellness
- Increased vitality
- Weight loss

Whether you want to lose weight, enhance sleep, reduce stress, build muscle or improve balance gentle chair yoga is the way to go. This book and audio teach you how.

Enjoy your chair yoga journey!

Florence Gauthier

ABOUT THE AUTHORS

Florence Gauthier

Florence is a Yoga and Pilates teacher who over the last decade has provided specialized chair and therapeutic yoga sessions for seniors to bring the benefits of yoga to those suffering from physical or cognitive impairment. Florence studied in Paris, Stockholm, and New York, and after many years in San Francisco now lives in Paris, the city of her birth.

David O'Connor

A fitness coach for 30 years, he has trained both seasoned athletes and beginners of all ages. David has authored several books with a mission to help seniors feel physically and mentally healthy, and designed to help seniors with muscle, joint, mobility, and flexibility problems. His maxim is "It's never too early to improve your fitness and never too late to start." David's mission is to assist elders with the increasing issues they face as they age. He is eager to demonstrate to them that they may take creative efforts to improve their fitness and live better lifestyles because he believes that things can be different.

David sought this book collaboration with Florence after he saw how her gentle yoga sequences helped his father move from a sedentary lifestyle to being back on the golf course and loving life again. David recognized that Florence's yoga sessions greatly improved his father's mental health, and instilled a sense of positivity that had been absent for many years.

Yoga warm-up and cool-down are now an integral part of David's training sessions. Seeing how his members respond to these sessions convinced him of the important part yoga plays in any structured fitness plan and especially those designed for seniors who are more susceptible to injury.

Leave a Review:

If you enjoy this book and it helps you achieve your goals, as I most definitely trust it will, please take a minute to leave a short Amazon review. Your feedback will help others considering starting their Chair Yoga journey.

SCAN TO LEAVE AMAZON REVIEW

FREE BONUS FITNESS MATERIAL TO HELP YOU ACHIEVE YOUR GOAL

To ensure you gain the most benefit from Chair Yoga for Seniors 50, 60 and Beyond we have included free access to the audiobook. It's a great companion, you don't have open the book and my students have reported that it helps them maintain motivation.

Your Bonus Materials

1) **Audio Book.** You can now enjoy the book almost anywhere simply scan QR code next to each chapter header.
2) **Video Guides.** You have lifetime access to our video library containing 60+ pose videos specifically recorded to help you maximise results.

   Simply follow the instructions on page 50 to gain access.
3) **4 Fitness Word Puzzles**. As a bit of fun to help maintain brain fitness too.
4) **Monthly Newsletter** on topics to help you succeed on your fitness journey.

GET YOUR FREE BONUS MATERIAL

INTRODUCTION

SCAN FOR AUDIO CHAPTER

"You are dozing off on that chair! You were safer on the couch." My exasperated daughter exclaimed, trying to hide the annoyance in her tone as she hurried out the door for a long day at work. Hurt and discouraged, I regretted having signed up for that chair yoga session down the street. She was worried that I would injure myself with a fall, but here I am, trying to build a healthy routine and seeming to go nowhere apart from looking ridiculous.

Well, that was me four years back. Yes, it was a low-spirited start. At five feet nine inches, weighing 207 lbs, and having worked 35 years as a research scholar with a 14-hour sedentary work routine, designing a robust post-retirement life was easier said than done. I didn't get it. I seemed to be doing all the right things. I prided myself in being a well-read person, would definitely not call myself lackadaisical, and I looked forward to living life hale and hearty going forward. However, it was irksome that apart from enjoying strolling in the community park in the mornings and evenings—which by the way got me in a good mood, since it was socializing and exercising rolled into one—I was not able to come to terms with anything on a higher plane as far as physical exercise was concerned. I was extremely cautious in the beginning of anything new. I had seen enough exercise-related injuries with my friends and acquaintances, and had sneered at their follies, so you wouldn't find me doing anything 'valorous' as such. I was to continue with my quest for a sensible form of exercise that I looked forward to continuing beyond the third day of beginning.

That's when I bumped into him at the bar. Dev Seth, my long-lost school buddy, was drinking, totally blissed out, and looking a decade and some younger than me. He had the same devilish smile, and seemed to sprint as compared to my drag. With formalities out of the way, I jumped into my question. "Ahem, do you exercise Dev?" "Well, I do." he responded.

He was very forthcoming. He understood my predicament and asked me to check out chair yoga. I hastened back home and gawked into Google ... 210 million results—I had no clue!

After 60 years of being a product of modern society, it hit me that we look at our bodies very differently. Educationist Ken Robinson made a poignant unsettling statement when he said that "we seem to use our bodies as a vehicle to transport our heads from one place to the other". (Robinson, 2006). That is how I had lived my life and now I want my body to dance to my tunes!"

When I first began my chair yoga practice, I approached it at the physical level, and I applied my entire focus towards achieving the perfect pose. I would grasp each posture at the intellectual level and expect my body to comply. After a day or two of stretching and bending, I began to suspect that my hands and legs had a mind of their own. They would refuse to listen to me, and protest by complaining of aches and pains or just by saying they didn't feel like it! I decided at that point that there was some investigation called for. Upon some probing and reading about yoga, I concluded that the missing puzzle piece was harmony. My mind and body had to come to terms with each other if I were to progress.

Why This Book

That was Victor, a client of mine, recollecting his experiences with us the other day. Upon hearing that it struck us how important it is to begin anything in the right frame of mind. We appear to allow misconceptions, patterns of thought, and dogma to limit our ability to achieve.

Another interesting issue we realized that was gnawing anyone eager to begin was the 'problem of plenty'. We would come across resources that had disjointed information that failed to empathize with the user. When the reader was looking for guidance on simple movements to help them go about their lives with dignity and happiness, information overload overwhelmed them with advice on intricate poses.

For the question as to what chair yoga is, you could get some answers and helpful videos on the internet, and in classes available in your neighborhood. However, you could end up with all the know-how of chair yoga, but soon find that you are not practicing it daily, or that it is a humdrum effort, and we dread that situation for anybody. Victor went through the agony of finding his progress stalling after the initial excitement. That stumped him and in turn, led us to pick up the missing pieces. More than anything, we are excited about sharing how chair yoga turned from a run-of-the-mill chore to an enchanting groove for Victor. Our objective with this book is to go beyond just providing information, we aspire to provide insights into what your chair yoga journey would look like.

This book is an effort to translate esoteric yoga principles into ones that can be adopted by regular people who are not familiar with traditional training. It will act as a constant and reliable companion to anyone who is set out to benefit from chair yoga. It endeavors to follow authoritative schools of Yoga and will not advise postures that are undefined by established schools. However, there is restraint exercised in terms of getting into philosophical discussions since the target audience are regular people taking baby steps. Using a chair as a prop is not intrinsic to traditional yoga practices and hence will call for some adaptations. This will mean keeping in mind safety aspects, and being mindful of unintended consequences such as long-term or short-term injuries. Sequencing a set of postures will also need customization that cannot be pre-determined in a simplistic fashion. After reading this book you will be able to determine your daily routine with a healthy dose of information and inspiration. A lot can be accomplished with small and consistent steps in shifting the mindset and nudging the body toward health. Reaching out to every kind of audience is indeed a happy challenge, and the focus of the book is on transformation by making yoga accessible, not merely giving information.

How to Use This Book and Things to Remember

The chapters are structured to introduce the reader to the WHAT, WHY, and HOW of chair yoga. In order to prevent one from missing out on important information about the goals of a posture in a particular chapter when going through the how-to's of the poses, we have attempted to disperse pertinent information throughout.

In each chapter, the name of the pose is followed in brackets by the Sanskrit name of the traditional '*yoga asana*', a name used in yoga for seated postures—in Sanskrit, the word 'asana' translates to 'seat'. The postures for chair yoga are inspired by the source yoga asanas, modified to adapt to the chair and needs of the practitioner. The purpose of mentioning the Sanskrit name of the source is for you to be able to trace it back to established forms for any deeper study.

The '*asanas*' are spread across the chapters to assist one in making a decision based on their priority and physical restrictions. The book will take you through the beginner's steps in an expansive and unhurried manner, before we get into postures that are more advanced.

The how-to steps are written with the goal of guiding you into the proper purpose and posture of the yoga asanas and at the same time be crisp in style. Therefore, when you read the phrase "take an upright position," it refers to performing the mountain pose elaborated in Chapter 5 in its full intent: with the body, mind, and spirit. If we didn't accomplish that, yoga would just be another style of calisthenics. If you notice that the directions occasionally become talk-heavy, we want you to appreciate that it is not to be bothersome; rather, it is to constantly remind us of the intentions behind each move.

Managing Physical Limitations And Concerns

We all have our bodily limitations, and yoga wants us to always be mindful of them. The central idea is to accept any hindrances with compassion and use the mind and spirit to address the situation. Struggling with seemingly simple things like not being able to keep your hands raised, being unable to twist your waist to the left, or a vague pain in your shoulders are perfectly normal situations irrespective of being young or old. At the end of the day, we are real people with our own sets of priorities and constraints. The objective of getting into chair yoga is to bring our awareness to it, and find solutions in the myriad range of *yoga asanas*.

We have time and again observed that yoga resources and trainers inadvertently give harmful cues or build fear through the language they use while discussing a pose. Always try out a posture with an attitude that your body will be able to take it. In case you find yourself inexplicably uncomfortable with a particular pose in terms of breathing or pressure exerted on any body part, you can stop right away, move on to another one, and revisit it sometime in the future. We have also restrained from casually using anatomical terms to avoid misinterpretation. If a particular instruction is giving you a funny feeling when you follow it, perhaps something has gotten lost in the language of the instructions. Always use your discretion.

A word on exercising caution: it is wise to avoid getting carried away into doing anything in excess just because it seems easy, as it will impede your progress and drive. Take guidance from an expert where you have to, and keep your doctor, therapist, and family in the loop with regular discussions of your progress and experiences. Achieving an organic evolution will be made easier by sticking to the procedures outlined in the book. If a particular posture seems out of your reach, that only means there are more options out there for you to explore. What matters is your willingness to try the variations of each move, and go through the process of acquiring it; the picture-perfect posture is a fantasy. Savor the delight of attempting them!

CHAPTER 1

The Fundamentals

Getting old is like climbing a mountain; you get a little out of breath, but the view is much better!

Ingrid Bergman

To Recognize What Is Not Yoga

If you believe otherwise, it is crucial to understand that yoga is not the same as exercise. How is this relevant? Well, it matters. Exercise is defined as a physically demanding activity done with the purpose of maintaining or enhancing fitness. This suggests that the emphasis is on using the body to develop it to meet your needs, and necessitates exercising control over the body through will and discipline. Yoga instead aims to control the mind and cultivate compassion and acceptance for the body, causing the body to obey your commands effortlessly. It adopts a unique perspective on well-being by not elevating the body above the mind. It is a curious case of shifting from effort to no effort, my friend! We should probably give some time for this idea to sink in, and so before pulling out that chair, we need to ponder this thought for a while.

A distinctive characteristic of yoga is its ability to put the practitioner in a state of mental and physical steadiness. It works on achieving stability and relaxation, while working on keeping the body-mind in optimum condition. It relaxes the muscles to increase flexibility, whereas most other regimes are aimed at flexing the muscles thereby reducing plasticity.

Unlike regular exercise regimens, there is no wear and tear of muscles, or exertion on the heart and lungs. The body naturally perceives exercise as stress and pumps out the stress neurotransmitter known as 'cortisol', whereas yoga relaxes the body by inducing the rest-relax state. What's more, the practice has a quintessential holistic approach, and generally frowns on the idea of working on isolated parts of the body.

Physical Fitness: A Consequence but Not the Goal of Yoga

Yoga is a Sanskrit word that was first mentioned in 'Rig Veda', an Indian philosophical text that dates back about 5,000 years. It is an ancient practice that was developed to bring about the integration of the mind, body, and spirit. It will surprise you that neither physical fitness nor weight loss was on the agenda. Self-realization is the aim of a yoga practitioner. In simple terms, it is to help anyone realize that they have infinite possibilities inside of them. Having said that, yoga, when adopted as a holistic practice in present times, will be the perfect answer to understanding yourself better and thus make it work towards enhancing your physical and mental fitness. It is a practice that is evolving and flourishing in all different corners of the world. Its unmatched approach makes it different from exercise routines such as aerobics, strength training, or swimming.

Yoga practitioners like to define yoga as a methodology that aligns the individual self with the universe, and here we need to decode this step by step starting with the body and mind. On the chair, with age being taken into consideration, we need to bring stability to the mind and body by adopting postures that will bring our awareness to our anatomical abilities' reality. The need is to be able to maintain a posture for a reasonable length of time by bringing one's consciousness to the body.

How Can Yoga Cut Any Ice

When you wake up in the morning, notice how your mind jumps into a train of thoughts. It could be a continuation of what you were contemplating the day before, or it might be about reminiscing or wondering about the future. By default, your mind is waiting to get on that train. If you have a rudimentary training in yoga, you would catch yourself thinking, and bring your mind back to the present. You would notice the sounds and sights around you, feel the ground beneath your feet, and take your attention to your breath. Aha, 'mindfulness' is the mantra you keep hearing from wellness coaches.

The first step, either with or without the chair, will be to practice the state of being without thought. That does not mean you stop thinking and force shut your brain. Trying that will only viciously invite more thoughts. It essentially means to be aware of what you are thinking, and then make sure that you bring yourself back to the present moment. Don't settle comfortably in that train of thought. Get in and get out to ensure you are going in the right direction. You surely would not mind the bonus of experiencing less anxiety, more energy to face challenges, and a better ability to go about the day.

Every time you set out to practice chair yoga and endeavor at it day in and day out, you must know that you are there to calm your mind, take control over your breath, love yourself, and be aware of your capabilities. We live life thinking that as individuals we hold no influence on family or society, we blame the government, and we are frustrated by the rot in institutions. Whether it is about keeping your table tidy or keeping the community clean, every time you breathe in, take in the freshness of possibilities, and when you exhale, let go of those conditioned thoughts that have been put into your mind by well-meaning parents, teachers, intellectuals, and friends. It is not about being idealistic, but you get the idea. Yoga is not just about making you fit, it is about unlocking more in yourself.

Anxiety, frustration, despondency, and other similar emotions are by-products of the industrial world, and are perpetually induced by the external environment. It is almost a default setting for many of us, and practicing yoga is inherently designed to develop the assurance that there are better options. Whether it is dealing with personal anxieties or more serious issues like post-trauma stress disorder (PTSD), the practice of yoga works on the mental and emotional levels by directing our thoughts and attention to intrinsic harmony. It works on the premise that we have innate capabilities to heal, and that it can be harnessed with the right practices.

Yoga is about looking inward as opposed to the popular culture of looking outwards for solutions to problems. The idea of being able to make friends with our bodies and minds is appealing. The restlessness of the mind and body is soothed by breathing techniques and body postures, and these techniques will nip a lot of issues in the bud. Hence, keep the faith and know that a lot is to be unraveled in the following days of practice.

Yoga as a Complementary and Remedial Therapy

Yogic practices were developed by the men of learning known as *rishis* in ancient India through millennia in their quest for liberation from suffering. The system as we know it today was compiled and systematized by the scholar and saint Patanjali in his classical work *Yoga Sutras*. It is a collection of 185 principles stated in a rather laconic style. Students of this collection have interpreted and developed different yogic systems over the centuries to enhance the spiritual, mental, and physical capabilities of its followers. With the unifying goal of managing life as effectively as possible, we find practitioners in numerous schools of yoga.

While we concentrate on the aspects of yoga that benefit our physical and mental health, it is helpful to remember that yoga is much more than this. It encourages moderation in daily activities such as eating and resting, as well as the control of the senses. It also aims to calm the mind and put it to rest so that wisdom can flow and delusions can fade. BKS Iyengar says in his seminal book *Light On Yoga*, that yoga is a technique for calming the racing mind and channeling agitated energy into constructive use.

It helps to know that a traditional 'yogi', as a yoga practitioner is called, will aspire to go through the eight stages of yoga that include ethical mandates, discipline for purification, body postures, breathing management, regulation of senses, concentration and meditation techniques, and attainment of a state of superconsciousness. Here we will be exploring two of the eight facets of yoga, which are yoga asanas or body postures, and a fundamental understanding of 'pranayama' or breath control.

Yoga is attracting the attention of medical professionals around the world due to its enormous legacy. In the realm of human wellness, it is currently a subject of significant debate and research. Although it has not yet been demonstrated to be a standalone treatment for many illnesses, it is unquestionably a crucial component of contemporary self-care behavioral therapy. It has shown psychophysiological advantages in controlling medical disorders such as high blood pressure, controlling distress, stroke after-effects, and other aging and lifestyle-related conditions.

How Often Is Chair Yoga to Be Practiced

Every time you sit in a chair—happy or grumpy, excited or sluggish—there is a posture for the occasion. It is a routine that can be spread throughout the day. One pose every time you sit down is an encouraging idea.

Post-65-year-olds will get the appropriate amount of strengthening and balancing exercises recommended by the Center For Disease Control and Prevention if they set aside time for practice for at least 15 minutes, three times each week. Yoga requires no special preparation because it is, by nature, in line with our existence. As a result, it is quite simple to include in daily life. Every time you practice, you will notice a sense of relaxation flowing through your body, thereby setting it up to ask for more.

No matter your age, even a 10 minute workout will unquestionably reap rewards for you. The great news is that studies have found that even occasional practice can have a noticeable, positive impact. The most important rule for choosing your optimal duration is to pay attention to your body and listen to its needs. So, where there is a chair, there is chair yoga.

CHAPTER 2

How Does Chair Yoga Work

The mind is like a parachute. It doesn't work if it is not open.

Frank Zappa

Knowing the Principles of Chair Yoga

Young people and golden-agers alike praise chair yoga for opening up a whole new universe of activities to maintain and improve mental and physical well-being. It is exceptional in that it is created to overcome physical and social restrictions of many different kinds. Chair yoga elegantly collects the wisdom traditional yoga has amassed over millennia and makes it available to anyone wanting to benefit from its practice. It provides solutions at a point where other exercise regimens start to falter. When a pupil most needs them, the teacher shows up. With its sophisticated approach to holistic care, yoga adheres to the maxim "less is more."

In the classical yoga asana discipline, there is a pose known as the 'chair pose' where one assumes the position of sitting on an imagined chair. Terri Guillemets, an Arizona-based quotation anthologist, hit the nail on the head when she said that the chair pose in yoga is "a defiance of spirit, showing how high you can soar even when you are forced down." (Asana – Inkpots & Daydreams). We believe this statement does a wonderful job of encapsulating the essence of chair yoga.

The journey of chair yoga as we know it began in 1982 in New York, when Lakshmi Voelker-Binder, an accomplished American yoga trainer, noticed her 30-something student struggling with yoga asanas because of arthritis. To help her draw the benefits despite her inability to sit on the ground or stand for a long time, Lakshmi used her mastery to develop postures for the chair. Her trademarked chair yoga program found takers all over the world, and has since opened up yoga to people with all kinds of physical limitations. There has been no looking back since then, and teachers and students across continents have helped the discipline evolve in its own right.

First things first—let us learn what chair yoga does for you.

It is Empathetic

It is effective as it is adopted with a Trauma-Informed Care approach where there is the presumption of a pre-existing medical condition. This approach ensures that the exercises are safe and hence will invite better adherence and consistency from the side of the practitioner. This also makes it crucial to stick to reliable sources of information, and not adapt anything sold in the name of chair yoga. In our years of providing training, and speaking with people who've experienced difficulties, the most common reason for giving up is the lack of an empathetic design in exercise progression. It is quite understandable that one does not want to take risks of short or long-term injuries at any age.

Therefore, chair yoga makes for an ideal program for anyone who looks forward to being enthusiastic about their workout every day, regardless of their medical history or previous lifestyle. It offers the benefits of any exercise regime along with being considerate and inexpensive. The cherry on top is that you will shatter preconceived notions about aging and inspire the community around you, most likely to the point you inspire them to join the movement.

Sets Up Mind-Body Balance

We cannot forget the grin on Henry's face when he was mentioning that he got an unexpected compliment, from of all people, his wife. Henry had this annoying quirk of invariably spilling water from the glass on the dining table whenever he picked it up. She couldn't help being exasperated since this habit was such a pain in the neck that she had endured for years.

One fine day his wife made this observation: "Henry, have you noticed that the water does not spill from your glass of late."

The benefits of doing chair yoga thus begin to reflect in very subtle ways that eventually have a huge bearing on the quality of our lives. It takes care of those undefinable aches, despondent moods, and the lethargy that clutches us silently. Days after starting chair yoga practice, we can't help noticing a smart difference in the way our yoga students behave, including how they walk, communicate, and build a resilient attitude.

Sleep Stories

A conversation among seniors is never complete without someone mentioning sleep deprivation. In recent memory, forced social distancing during the Covid-19 pandemic had many of us take solace in the digital screen. This, in turn, led to overstimulating the part of the mind that gravitated toward negative emotions more often than not. Chair yoga has proven to be a savior in resetting our biological rhythms and helping us rejuvenate.

When we talk about sleep we are essentially talking about the quality, because feeling disturbed and unrested even after long hours of dozing does not hack it. In its article on Yoga and Sleep, The Sleep Foundation found that 85% of study participants reported less stress, thus they project an increased sleep efficiency in 55% of yoga practitioners. This elaborates on how the elderly populations face sleep disturbances like insomnia, snoring, and restless leg syndrome, and reports an improvement in these conditions when yoga is practiced.

The assuring news is that long-term practitioners score better in sleep quality. The deep breathing practices of yoga activate the parasympathetic nervous system, inducing a relaxed sleep. It becomes easy to develop optimum sleep hygiene with a good daytime routine. For most of our lives, sleep came to us naturally and hence was presumed to stay with us, but as we grow older it seems to need an appointment to come over. Modern society has firmly reached a stage where it is time for us to take an earnest look at educating ourselves on sleep.

Is Energy Efficient

It is with great joy Martin announced that his physics brain had observed that his chair yoga exercises are energy efficient. He explained how his old life gyming regimen had needed him to build and conserve energy to ensure sustenance. He spent his days counting calories, and the exercises resulted in the targeted development of muscles by allocating resources to certain body parts. There is an increase in blood pressure during exercise and the muscles are torn to develop them.

Chair yoga works on a completely different paradigm. It develops muscles evenly all over, the body is relaxed, and blood flow is regulated once you attain the correct posture. You will not find your heart strained in any of the poses and to boot, there is no fatigue that a normal exercise induces due to lactic acid creation. Yoga is anabolic with slow movements conserving energy, whereas exercises are catabolic since they demand forceful movements that use up a lot of calories. It will not necessitate you to take health supplements to sustain yourself.

Its Effect On Mental Health

If you like to have an academic understanding of how yoga practice helps mental health, there are research results to draw your interest. Regular yoga practice that includes breathing exercises has been proven to help in addressing fatigue in normal people as well as patients undergoing long-term treatment for cancer, asthma, and dialysis. Research using electrophysiological markers of attention and increasingly sophisticated brain research advancements are giving us a clearer picture of how breathing techniques affect patients with clinical depression. Yoga interventions have shown effectiveness in research trials, and are sustaining the interest for deeper study.

In a study published in 2017 by Stanford Research Institute, Mark Krasnov* and his colleagues discovered a small cluster of neurons that connected breathing to calmness, focus, enthusiasm, and anxiety. It enables people all over the world to comprehend how breathing exercises function at the cellular and molecular levels.

It effectively recognizes and addresses the feeling of lack of meaning as a fundamental cause of sadness that leads to further breakdown of other functions of the mind. Anecdotes of practitioners of yoga have time and again demonstrated a cognitive restructuring of the brain to help reclaim well-being.

Richard J Davidson, psychologist and neuroscientist, explains how using modern scientific tools to study kindness and compassion as against only probing the effects of anxiety and depression on the human brain can give clues to path-breaking solutions. An important insight in his study was the ability of anyone to take responsibility for the changes happening in our ever-changing brain. Apparently, we spend 47% of our time not focused on work. We are becoming increasingly lonely as we, as individuals indulge more in negative self-talk than the previous generation. Simple actions that increase our awareness, embrace mindfulness, show compassion for ourselves and others, and help increase our insight and purpose are certainly within our reach.

Flexibility: Your New Friend

Every time we stretch, our muscle groups, joints, and connective tissues are activated and they expand to achieve their full range of motion. The American College of Sports Medicine recommends stretching major muscle groups at least twice a week to maintain flexibility in movement (American College of Sports Medicine, 2022). Our bodies are designed for mobility, and stiffness creeps in every time we underuse any of our muscles, and age can be a contributing factor to taking sedentary positions.

We achieve what is known as a 'static stretch' by stretching and holding it for a few seconds. This will surely help us observe the body's responses, but a dynamic stretch where we don't hold it is just as beneficial. Yoga trainers, however, believe that extended holding provides more long-lasting flexibility. It is important to keep in mind that stretching should give a feeling of unwinding and not pain. Not to forget that in yogic terms flexibility goes beyond physiology and applies to attitude as well.

A contributing cause for losing flexibility is the loss of hydration in the tissues which causes it to lose its suppleness. Stretching helps by stimulating the production of tissue lubricants. Movements warm up the body and thus help build elasticity. When you are able to hold your poses for a longer duration, you know that your flexibility has improved, and it also becomes our responsibility to not cause damage by overdoing them. In his article What Every Yogi Needs To Know About Flexibility, Fernando Pages Ruiz* elaborates on the scientific research and anecdotal reports going into understanding how flexibility is impacted by yoga asanas (2021).

Improved Strength

A strong core is highly desirable in old age to avoid injuries. Most falls are avoidable if the gait and balance are addressed through regular yoga practice. A lot of us prefer remaining seated safely on a couch to avoid mishaps and this only triggers more possibilities of falls.

Every pose in this book will help strengthen your muscles and reduce the likelihood of falls. It is self-assuring to be able to go about independently with our activities and leisure, and is an attainable goal as we wage the gentle war to keep our dignity intact.

A Significant Improvement in Self Awareness

Whether we are exercising or not, the body coordinates its movements every time we change positions by gauging its presence in terms of space, distance, and speed. We incur the risk of falling, spraining, or twisting if we don't have control of this harmony. Tara Fraser, yoga teacher and author of *Yoga For You* likes to say that yoga is essentially a practice for your soul, working through the medium of your body (2003) . The point is that we do not address body issues at the level of the body alone. The anatomy of the body is subject to self-awareness and yoga practice lends itself beautifully to increasing this cognizance.

Much-Needed Reduction in Stress

Chair Yoga practice is akin to moving meditation as it encourages heightened awareness coupled with slow deliberate movements that will regulate the release of stress hormones in the body. The body gets into stress mode with every worry and anxiety that society contributes in the form of work issues, health troubles, financial constraints, and relationship management. We feel constantly under attack, which in turn gets the body on overdrive with increased heart rate and blood pressure, and energy expenditure. If you find yourself getting easily startled or anxious while going about daily tasks, it is time to draw your attention to the breathing techniques that should be part of your chair yoga sessions. The slowdown and take-charge mode of yoga serves as an immediate solution for both the short and long-term capacity to manage pressures.

According to a 2014 study by Stanford scholar Emma Seppala, breathing meditation significantly assisted army veterans in managing post-traumatic stress disorder (PTSD) when medicine and conventional therapy had failed. Coupled with the fact that the United States Defense Department* (TEDx Talks, 2015) uses yoga today to assist veterans and train their navy SEALS says something about the reputation of yoga. The United States sadly loses roughly 20 veterans to suicide each day (Monson, n.d.) and so a breakthrough is major news. If this can be replicated to address daily stressors we are talking huge numbers.

When Pain Pounces

Pain and even anticipation of pain can be overwhelming factors for us as we age. It is only fair that we are prepared to take charge of the situation even before it arises. It is accepted knowledge that exercise boosts the release of endorphins and other pain-relieving chemicals. Additionally, yoga addresses pain by including layers of characteristics such as deep breathing to bring awareness to painful areas, inviting acceptance of the situation, and practicing the idea that the pain will leave your body with certain practices.

CHAPTER 3

What Chair Yoga Does to You

Strength doesn't come from what you can do. It comes from overcoming the things you once thought you couldn't.

—Ashley Greene

We need to know the answers to our many questions and concerns about an appropriate yoga plan. A conversation on how chair yoga can provide creative solutions to living an enthusiastic life despite difficulties will help us unravel the strategies in simple ways. The simplest starter being the chair, it is the accessibility to the opportunity of exercising that does not fail to amaze us. Grab a chair anywhere you go: the doctor's waiting area, the park bench, at the church, in the restaurant, and you can do a posture that makes you happy.

Who Should Do Chair Yoga

Suitable for All Ages Especially the Elderly

Performing yoga postures with the aid of a chair is a game-changer that will help many of us cross over from limitations to huge possibilities since the chair is the most non-threatening place one can think of to do some exercise. Our limitations are not restricted to the frailties of natural aging. Seniors watch out, you will have stiff competition here. It is with alarm that we see cascading effects of ill health on people in their prime age. Long hours at the desk in the office are taking a toll, causing backaches, muscle cramps, stiff necks, and burnouts as a consequence of popular high-demand, competitive, and ruthless work environments. Anyone from caregivers, to new mothers, farmers, executives, and even adolescents living in high-stress conditions today are advised to adopt chair yoga.

In case you are looking out for a post-retirement plan like Victor, nothing could be more tailor-made for you. It is customizable, not difficult, and encourages healthy aging. If you are a person who has been in top shape during your younger years, chair yoga is still an option because we have seen former athletes stumped on a chair when they realize they are activating certain muscle groups for the first time ever.

For Anyone With Mobility Issues

We all feel the need to take extra care as age advances. Fragility is natural and one needs to work with it. Yoga by nature is diverse and thus offers something for everyone. Chair yoga allows one to work on themselves without the need to be in a peak state of fitness. As long as you can sit, you can make the most of it. It is indeed assuring to read medical journals wherein trials have shown patients overcome the fear of falling when exposed to chair yoga therapy. Due to the impairments in mobility caused by multiple sclerosis and spinal cord injuries, careful body coordination becomes essential. Yoga poses provide a starting point for the handling adjustments that are required.

To Fight Obesity

Obesity in old age and youngsters is the top psychological inhibition to begin exercising, apart from the fact that it is a major contributing factor to other lifestyle diseases. Yoga is an inviting proposition that will not judge you and also help you accept your body with compassion. And to know that the possibility of failure is nil. Since the postures are all essentially low impact, it helps in keeping the motivation high with each progressing session. Adding light weights for additional resistance while doing the postures will particularly help burn excess calories. Increasing anecdotal reports have strengthened the case of chair yoga for anyone with an obesity challenge.

To Address the Fear of Falling

We may not admit it or even realize it, but if we have to point to one reason that haunts us as we age it is the fear of falling. A study of the effects of chair yoga therapy on physical fitness in patients with psychiatric disorders in a 12-week controlled trial* brought forth the observations that it improved physical fitness and effectively addressed the fear of falling (Schmid et al., 2010).

Falls in older people are common and prove costly if you ask people at the Center for Disease Control and Prevention. It reports 36 million falls among older adults every year* that result in head injuries and broken bones. However, the good news is that it goes on to say that falls are not an essential part of aging and are preventable (*Older Adult Falls | Fall Prevention | Injury Center | CDC*, 2022). It is important to observe your movements, and report to your doctor when you observe any tendencies to trip, dizziness, vision issues, or side effects of medication. Apart from this, keeping your strength and balance intact with chair yoga is a smart move to make.

For Those With Specific Medical Conditions

Stroke And Paralysis Recovery

There is a lot of interest in understanding the causes of strokes and what a layman could do to prevent them. A stroke is a kind of brain attack that happens when the blood flow stops in some areas due to clotting or an artery rupture. This results in parts of the brain cells dying which would temporarily or permanently cause immobility in related body parts, or memory loss. According to the Centers for Disease Control and Prevention, this has become one of the leading causes of death and disability in developed countries, with at least 795,000 people* suffering a stroke in the USA every year (CDC, 2019).

An 8-week 16-session observatory study of yoga therapy in stroke patients* conducted to understand its effects on pain, strength, endurance, and range of motion produced encouraging results. It showed improvement in multiple areas of physical functioning and is hence recommended as a complementary intervention to traditional rehabilitation (Lai et al., 2022).

Correlations between yoga practices and stroke prevention and recovery are a buzzing area of research with new insights coming in regularly. Yoga has found acceptance as part of occupational therapy to enhance the benefits of medical treatment. It works on addressing long-term disability caused by strokes by improving mobility and strength. It does so by working at the physical level, and also improving the ability of the brain to make new connections and adapt to changing needs.

Speaking to stroke survivors who have benefitted from chair yoga therapies has helped us gain insights into their experiences. The simplicity of chair yoga practice makes it something for them to look forward to. A recent study* also concluded that yoga can be used as a self-administered practice in stroke rehabilitation since the trial demonstrated reduced anxiety levels along with physical improvement (Lai et al., 2022). An intrinsic part of stroke therapy is the need to establish the lost connection between the body and mind and this is where the gentle and deliberate movements of yoga prove useful.

Preventing and Managing Dementia

Dementia is a cognitive disorder with no known cure, but managing its symptoms and preventing an onset is definitely a paramount aspect in our interests. It is a condition that has a significant impact on the morale of the patient and family as well.

Breathing exercises influence the nervous system and work on lifting the mood, self-regulating emotions, and engaging parts of the brain that stimulate neuroplasticity. Research has shown how mindfulness causes less atrophy in the hippocampus, thus reducing cognitive decline. Chair yoga encourages patients to practice postures that offer a variety of possibilities since it enhances body awareness and attention, which will help them become more alert when managing their daily routine.

CHAPTER 4

Caveats And Cautions To Be Exercised In Chair Yoga

Each day is another chance to change your life.

Unknown

Preparations for a chair yoga routine are incomplete unless we get a complete picture of what the practice will look like for us. It is worth spending time contemplating some of the things that can go wrong in order to empower ourselves and avoid anything that causes pain, injury, or demotivation. We recommend that you speak to your physician and physiotherapist before starting, especially if you have a history of medical issues and in order to keep yourself alert to misinformation.

A five-minute everyday routine will work, to begin with, if you want unceasing benefits. The body will train itself to persist with the stretches and bends and you find yourself sitting longer each progressing session. We want an organic progression and there are no deadlines to meet. Never forget that yoga is possible as long as you have a chair to sit on, so you always have a variety of postures to choose from.

When There Is Undue Strain

We must accept the physical limitations of the body regardless of our age. Stressing the system is different from gently nudging it. The brain will go into alert mode as soon as there is any such strain, and the next thing you know, you are being forced to drag yourself to the next practice session. Unlike at the gym, let us not forget that a chair yoga session is the one place you will get brownie points for staying relaxed. Make the most of it.

Showing impatience and rushing through the stages will turn chair yoga into mere antics. Your basic mountain pose will appear to be achieved by sitting upright on the chair. However, executing it involves mental focus, getting the emotional frame right, paying complete attention to the body, and focusing on breathing techniques. Each stage requires a consistent rewiring of our intellect and training of the body to follow suit. We cannot forget the fact that society has ensured that our default is set to rushing mode. Eat faster, score higher, and achieve better have been the tone throughout our childhood and adulthood, and it's high time we reclaim our bliss. We don't have to go faster, we just need to keep at it—the key to success here is consistency.

We get it when you feel frustrated every time you see your yoga buddy or that more senior neighbor getting that perfect pose. It is fine to try and reach perfection but it is important not to obsess over it or get fixated on targets. You will not get a medal for flawlessness, but enjoying the process will fetch you many bonuses.

Recognize Bad Pain

We must learn to respond differently when pain results from the awakening of the muscles as opposed to when the discomfort is a warning of damage. Pay attention to your gut feeling or discuss with a trained practitioner if you have consistent aches that do not disappear with the progression of practice. A jerky movement when you transit through movements is unacceptable in yoga. If you are expected to raise your hands, it is to be done ever so gently even if you feel it's easy-peasy.

As one progresses through the various postures, it is important to understand the contraindications of each of them. For instance, twisting postures would not be a good idea for those with spinal cord injuries, and forward bends will cause discomfort when you have hip weakness. Since chair yoga in itself is low impact, a commonsensical understanding of what you can and cannot do at a given point will carry you safely through your practice.

Soreness in the muscles is caused due to lactic acid build-up during exercise. To counter the pain you will need to stretch mindfully. Lack of synovial fluids in the joints also causes discomfort and it should reduce when you continue to practice to keep the movement alive. If you find the soreness persisting or increasing in spite of this, it is time to visit the doctor.

Timing of Exercise

In terms of the clock, an early morning or late evening routine is recommended for traditional yoga asana. Chair yoga however gives us the anytime-anywhere luxury. Feel free to indulge when you feel like it.

Now that we have a perspective on how yoga differs from traditional physical exercise routines, plan a daily schedule that works for you. Having to keep your eyes wandering around to stare down at your grandkid to silence her is not exactly the ideal time. Sally likes to start her day with yoga as soon as she gets out of bed since at other times she finds her daily routine distracting to both her attention and willpower. As the day progresses, cooking, shopping, visiting, and screen time seem more important than needing to spend some time on self-care.

Busy days seem to have the power to draw us toward the outside world and tempt us to forget our personal needs. However, we also have the likes of our new student Jerry, who prefers getting his daily obligations done with enough time so that he can devote to working on himself. It is a choice that needs to be made with a healthy dose of self-love in mind.

The asanas are best done on an empty stomach. That does not imply that one should be hungry either. Waiting for at least an hour after a meal is beneficial since less energy will be used for food digestion than when the activities are done shortly after a large meal. Stay hydrated and remember to keep drinking water handy to sip at intervals; the mind will stay alert and exhibit determination if these aspects are taken care of.

The postures have an effect on internal organs as well. Our bodies' built-in defense mechanism is to hold off on further activity for a few hours after eating, but we seem to have learned to stop paying attention to this cue. Similar to how our stomachs tell us to stop eating when we're full, and we ignore them since we're either binging on the food, lost in thought, or otherwise preoccupied with talking or watching TV.

Warming Up and Cooling Down

Yoga is gentle, but some warm-up is still warranted. Stiffness comes complimentary with age and it will help to give mild rotating tasks to the wrists and neck, bends to the back, and stretches to the arms and legs. In any case, the body is stiffer in the mornings due to the hours of rest it had during the night. Relaxing post asanas are also called for even though we are not straining. Cooling down techniques that involve a few moments of silence and contemplation will help us mentally and physically transition to our normal routine after a session of chair yoga.

Existing Injuries and Conditions

Disturbing a body part that is already injured or recovering from surgery is not called for under any circumstance.

Learn to listen to the body because every pose should provide a sense of vitality and if your body says otherwise, it calls for a relook.

Begin to Notice Patterns and Attend to It

If you have ever got an absurd feeling during practice that the pose is not seeming right, then you are right. Listen to your body to adjust the pose, and if you feel tempted to give up, go ahead. But not without reminding yourself that moving is always a better choice than not moving, even if it is sometimes imperfect. There is nothing to fret about, because as we progress we will begin to notice our tendencies to retract to the wrong postures and we will learn to correct them. We will, for instance, realize that we kept our shoulders spread out initially with instruction but unknowingly let them droop midway. Similarly, the spine may bend or we could unwittingly throw our weight to one side of the hip.

Being creatures of habit, these are patterns set into us over time, so it helps to bring compassionate attention to how our bodies feel during the asana and nudge them back to the ideal position. Use tips like keeping your eyes open and watching yourself in a mirror during the initial practices of any new pose. Then, move on to do them with your eyes closed for better concentration and mindfulness. We also need to remember that the beginning and end of any posture cannot be abrupt, and not to push to the point of pain; instead, hold the pose and breathe. Begin with small, easy steps and watch the ordinary turn into the extraordinary.

Equipment and Other Resources to Use

The Chair

A visit to an African or Asian countryside house will find you looking around, wondering where to sit. A chair is still a fancy non-essential piece of furniture for many a society. The ground is good enough to rest your buttocks on or to get into the squatting position to eat or start a conversation. Well, the lesson learned here is that the body has sufficient mechanisms to take care of itself. I find this perspective important to anyone starting on the journey of chair yoga. The chair is, of course, a useful invention and will be a pivot in helping us get our act together. It is going to be your partner in progress, almost a soul mate in the journey.

The chair is a great tool to help you remain seated during yoga to provide stability and balance. It will help to overcome the limitations of inflexibility, injury, and imperfect body balance. It helps to slow you down and avoid rash movements. The conventional asanas can be performed standing up, or while seated on a mat on the floor. Since it supports the back and enables the body to hold positions much longer, the chair will help us gain the full benefits of the asanas. In some of the postures, one would even use the chair for support while standing or resting on the floor. Just like a kid learning to ride a bicycle, it will also help you remain enthusiastic and eagerly look forward to the next round of practice. With abandon, allow the chair to help you meander the postures for health and happiness.

The chair has to be of minimalist design with a straight back and light cushioning that is firm and not too soft. Make sure it is sturdy because a chair that moves around is sure to cause injury at some point. It should not have hand rests, as they do not allow for hand movements and bending. Due to their occasionally flimsy nature, convenient plastic chairs do not meet this requirement, nor are office chairs with wheels safe for seniors. A dining chair design is great since the seat is not caved in for lounging and normally has a weight-bearing capacity. The floor or ground should have enough friction to keep the chair stable. A park bench is just as fine to do your stretches - you'll have difficulty finding excuses for not starting. The exercises are to be done barefoot for best results, and a yoga mat under the feet and chair can take care of cold floors. You want the mat to stay firm to ensure there is no tripping over it; wear cotton socks if you wish. In case you want to wear shoes, they need to be the athletic kind that can stretch and are made of breathable material.

The practice of chair yoga requires little room. Contrary to traditional yoga, which requires some floor space to find stability and ease in every posture, having limited space is not a problem, just that you will have to see that there is enough space to fully extend your body. The beauty is that a chair can fit in where a mat cannot.

Wheelchairs and Power Chairs

People with any form of disability that can sit can benefit from chair yoga, even if it is a wheelchair. Chair yoga really is a tremendous equalizer and confidence booster accessible to all!

It is important to make sure that the wheels are locked in and the floor is non-slip. Ensure you have access to help in case of an emergency and things should be fine. Since being in a wheelchair is confining in itself, the idea of it being your accessory for exercising is truly freeing. The postures will remove the stiffness from hours of sitting and ensure healthy blood circulation. It will tone the abdominal region, the pelvic floor, and internal organs to give you the benefit of movement.

Clothing and Accessories

Choosing clothes with a comfortable fit that aren't too tight or loose is an important aspect for a hindrance-free practice. The body will warm up as you proceed, so you will need to layer accordingly. Before you sit down for a practice session make sure to take off spectacles, chains, and bands to avoid them falling, getting caught in clothing, and causing jerky movements due to such disturbances.

Yoga Blocks

It is a good idea to have blocks and straps to aid us to enhance the benefits of the postures. We see a lot of practitioners reluctant to use them since it feels dependent like a crutch, whereas it is not.

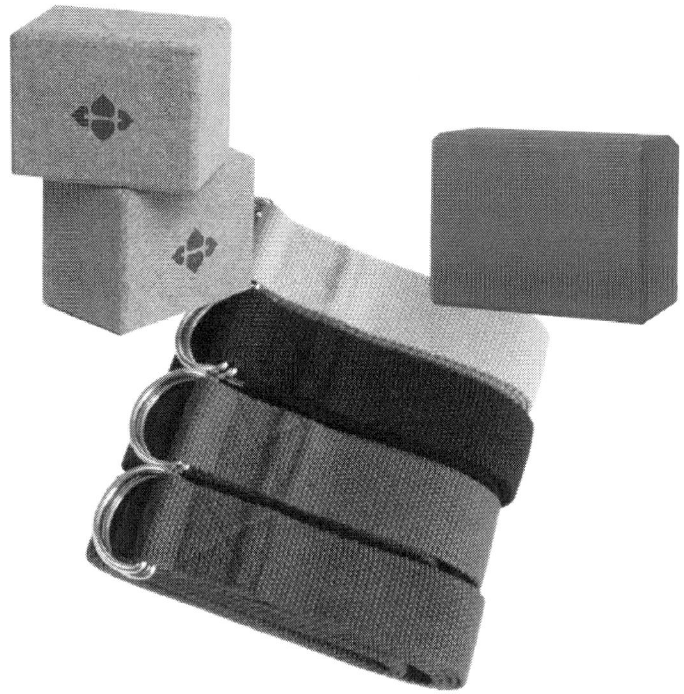

They are absolutely legitimate aids for getting better results and are inexpensive to purchase. Have these props handy so that you can use them without having to go fetch them in the middle of practice.

Yoga blocks or bricks help in resting the feet when you find it difficult to reach them to the ground during certain poses like stretches and lunges; they account for differences in symmetry and proportion. They can also be placed in between the knees to maintain posture during upper body twists. When you have not yet reached the flexibility needed for a pose, these bricks come in handy. You do not have to worry about becoming dependent on them, since it is more important to give those movements to the body rather than opting to skip them because of discomfort. Have at least two blocks handy when you begin your session. There are flat, medium, and tall ones available for you to choose from, depending on your needs.

Yoga Straps

When we struggle with tight hamstrings and shoulders, straps can come to the rescue. Looping a strap around your feet will help you bend forward or reach your feet. It is helpful to move the shoulders back and forth when held up and stretched. Lightweight dumbbells are handy to use during warm-ups, but use them with caution, as they can hurt if dropped by accident. Straps are your best bet since they give you the benefit of dumbbells in strength training without risk of injury.

Pillows and Blankets

Blankets are useful to place under the glutes to help the pelvis get into a comfortable position, as sitting for long periods can strain the sitting bones. The padding provided by the blanket will help you sustain and benefit from more postures. A pillow is useful to keep on your lap to rest your arms upon, or to lay your chest on during forward bends.

CHAPTER 5

Your Very First Lesson to Get Started With Chair Yoga

SCAN FOR AUDIO CHAPTER

Beautiful young people are accidents of nature, but beautiful old people are works of art.

—Eleanor Roosevelt

Adopting the Accurate Sitting Position

Alright! Now that you have earned yourself a chair, let's begin with the fundamental yoga positions. Since the sitting pose is the primary stance on which everything in chair yoga rests, we are actually going to sit down for a heart-to-heart conversation now.

The upright position in which we normally sit takes the avatar of the Mountain Posture in chair yoga. The mountain posture will appear to us as well, just somebody sitting smartly on a chair. Yet it is the supreme foundation upon which all else will thrive. We can still be left with something after writing an entire thesis on the mountain posture.

To put things in perspective:

- Time taken for assuming a sitting position is typically 4 seconds.
- Time taken for assuming the mountain posture is typically 30-40 seconds.
- This is not because it is slow, but rather because it is deep.

We invite you to read up the mountain posture time and again to help internalize it in all its glory. When you come back to it as you practice, you will find it revealing its layers of wisdom to you each time.

The Worth of Weight Distribution

It is a fact that most of us do not pay attention to our basic standing and sitting posture. Notice how we impose our body weight either on one leg, certain edges of the heels, or slouch to disturb the spine's optimum bearing. Observe how your shoes tend to get worn out at particular angles and you will know what we are talking about. A fundamental mastery of the sitting position is critical to regaining and maintaining body balance and gait. Tightness in the hamstrings or hip can make it difficult to keep the back straight. Fret not and keep the body gently moving to get back its flexibility. Start working on your posture and you will see the cascading effect it has in the days to come. Pay attention to it while at a friend's birthday party, or waiting at the ticket counter, you will start feeling stronger and also begin noticing the appreciative glances it draws.

A correct posture is the starting point for the agility of the body and mind, building elasticity of the spine, and the firming of thigh, stomach, and chest muscles. A slouched back and protruded stomach is never an aspiration surely. Practice keeping the correct posture to prevent unwarranted straining and it helps to remember that this will have a direct bearing on our personality, self-esteem, and people's perception of us.

The Prime Pose of Chair Yoga: The Mountain Posture

If you master this, you have conquered the mountain! It is to be perpetually kept in mind that we are delving into two facets of yoga throughout our workout journey. They are body postures or *yoga asanas* or just *asanas* as we refer to them, and breathing discipline or *pranayama*. The *asanas* have evolved to address different parts of the body, muscles, even internal organs, and glands, and also soothe the nerves. Paying attention to breathing or intentional breathwork complements the asanas to ensure a calm state of mind and intellect.

We shall together explore the most fundamental yoga asana, which is called Tadasana or the Mountain Posture. This posture is seemingly simple yet the most profound. Consider the serene motionless strength of a mountain. It stands tall unaffected by the upheaval of the world; one would not find it perturbed and clamoring to stay relevant. Likewise, we will reclaim our mental, spiritual and physical vigor with the most important of the series of asanas.

Complimentary Video Library Access

As a thank you for purchasing Chair Yoga For Seniors 50, 60 and Beyond you have lifetime access to the Chair Yoga Video Library.

To register:

Scan for Videos Access

or in your web browser enter https://www.iaa.pub/chair-yoga-join

The videos have been specifically recorded to accompany the book and are invaluable reference if you are unsure how to perform a pose correctly.

The Mountain Posture (Tadasana) #1

Preparation:

Take a seat and feel the texture of the chair. Be in the present, and direct your awareness to your legs, abdomen, spine, hands, and every other part of the body. Be in complete acceptance and compassion of your physical form and feel gratitude for the support it provides you. Discern the bliss that a child feels on discovering the miracles of what its hand and legs can do and make that feeling your own. Extend this awareness outside the body. In fact, feel one with the chair as if it were your body part. Now extend this emotion to the things in your immediate environment, then to those that are far away, and finally to everything in the cosmos. You will begin to experience integrity you haven't felt before.

How-to:

Scan For Audio

1) Sit back into the chair until the seat is completely supporting your glutes and hamstrings and stop sliding back at the point where the feet are comfortably resting on the floor. Make sure your back is not touching the backrest. Allow the legs to remain slightly apart so that they are at hip distance and parallel to the chair's legs as well as each other. Straight ahead should be the toes' natural position. Focus on the toes by softly spreading them out on the floor. The metatarsals and heels should be firmly rested. Use blocks under your legs if you cannot get the feet to rest on the floor without hurting your hips or back, it is just as fine. Adjust your seating to check for body weight distribution since it is important to have the weightiness distributed on the legs and not just the hips.
2) Tuck the stomach in so that the muscles of the thighs firm up too. The glutes have to press gently into the chair seat to keep the muscles taut. Let your arms hang down straight by your sides with your palms facing inwards while you settle your posture.

3) Now gently place both your arms on the thighs towards the knees with palms facing up as if to receive the energy from the universe. The palms need to be relaxed, unlike the feet which have to be rooted firmly to the ground.

4) Make sure the chest is drawn forward, the shoulders are pulled back straight, and the neck is upright. In order to achieve the posture, it is a good idea to warm up the body once in a while during the process. Rotate your wrists, move around the shoulders, rub your arms or legs; and get back to maintaining the posture. Go on and be alive to the process, it does not have to be a somber one.

5) Once done, have a soft gaze that looks straight ahead into the vastness. Alternatively, you could bring the chin down and gaze at the open palms, or keep the eyes closed to focus on your breath.

6) In your mind observe with compassion the soles feeling the ground, all of your body beginning with the legs, moving to the torso, and finally to the crown of your head.

7) Observe your breath and allow the inhalation and exhalation to get a little deeper than you normally do. Inhale, hold and exhale twice as long as the inhalation. Do not force any breathing pattern, just notice it. The intent here is to completely soak in the experience of our body and mind and feel the connection to the ground beneath and the space around us. If the mind begins to get restless or wander, do not resist. Allow all positive, negative, lovable, and hateful thoughts to get in as they occur. All you have to do is observe, acknowledge, and seek their departure when they enter. Welcome, and let go; whether the thoughts are ravages of the past or anxieties of the future, or delightful ones, gaze at them, but do not hold on and stare.

8) Hold the position for a while. Open your eyes and relax.

Mastering the mountain pose will teach us the nuances of the physical and emotional condition to adopt throughout any asana practice, asking you to maintain this frame of mind throughout all of your asanas, no matter how big or small, and eventually in all you do. By adopting this position, we can achieve emotional equilibrium, an ideal gait, optimal weight distribution, and correction of our posture, which has been negatively impacted by years of either being preoccupied with work or just not paying attention to it.

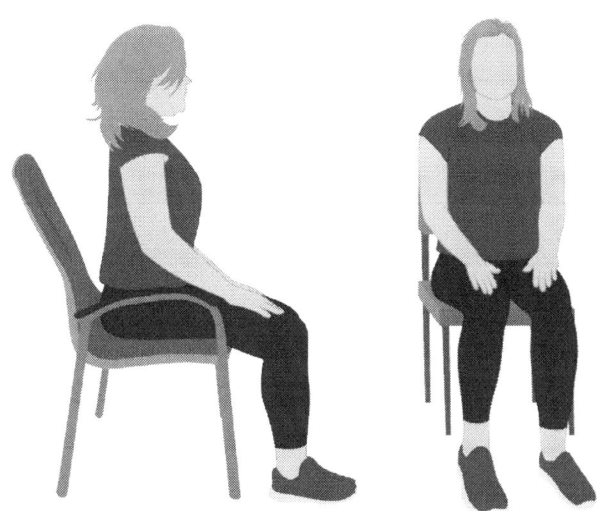

Efficient Ways to Move Your Body

At the body level, we are a combination of external and internal organs that are prone to environmental influences, there is the blood that needs to be at optimum pressure levels, hormones that are induced by various cues, a complex and sensitive nervous system, and cells that have withstood the test of time, and much more as we dig deeper. A rudimentary understanding of our ever-changing bodies will help us respect their needs and keep them in form.

Once you are seated on the chair it is a good idea to start with warm-up moves. These moves will give you an instant indication of your body's readiness. Be gentle with your movements at all times. Sit upright on your chair with your back straight and shoulders spread out. Keep your legs at a right angle to the ground with your soles firmly feeling the ground. The stomach should be tucked in and the buttock muscles taut. The hands are to rest palms downwards on the knees. You can hold on to the sides of the chair if you wish to.

Circles to Start Warm Up

How-to:

Scan For Audio

Raise your feet a little above the ground and rotate them in opposite directions for up to 10 counts. Change directions and continue for another 10 counts. This relieves stiffness and lubricates the joints and shins to kick start into action. You can start with one leg at a time if you so wish. Bring your attention to your breathing periodically. Swing your legs up and down gently, feel good for no reason and now proceed to repeat this rotation with the wrists and then move on to the shoulders. The neck will need to be warmed up with gentle turns in the left-to-right and top-to-bottom directions, and then by drawing imaginary circles with your nose in both directions. No, we have not advised an owl rotation!

See-Saw Feet Warm Up

How-to:

Scan For Audio

This warm-up exercise is sure to get your ankles up and about. Sit upright and slowly raise your heels with your toes firmly on the ground. Hold for a few seconds and feel the ankles and calf muscles awaken. Rest the heels back and raise the metatarsals and toes. Hold and repeat this seesaw a few times. Now raise your feet to about knee level. Take care not to raise them higher than knee level, as that could put you out of balance. Now stretch your legs so that your toes point upward to the sky. Inhale deeply and hold. Now exhale longer and simultaneously point your toes forward, then repeat. This warm-up will get you ready for your asanas.

The Lazy Stretch Warm Up

How-to:

Scan For Audio

You will have noticed how the body wants to stretch when we keep it in sedentary positions, for instance, when on a desk job for hours. We will adopt this natural tendency to develop some stretching variations for warming up.

Sit in an upright position and raise both arms towards the front at chest level. Clasp both palms together and interlock the fingers. Turn the wrists so that the palms turn away from you. Stretch your arms as if you are pushing away an object from you. Keep the arms parallel to the ground always. Hold for about ten seconds and pay attention to your breathing when waiting. Release and repeat if you feel tension in the wrists or forearms. After a few reps slowly raise your hands over your head with the fingers remaining interlocked and palms facing the sky. Hold and breathe for about ten seconds. Slowly bend rightwards and then on to the left. Get back straight, unlock the fingers and bring your hands to rest on the knee. This beautifully relaxes the entire spine, shoulders, hip muscles, and arms.

Cat-Cow Stretch (Marjaryasana-Bitilasana) #2

This combination posture will help relax your spine and is a wonderful introduction to body movement and breathing coordination. Think of a cow with its head looking upward, navel pushed outwards and buttocks pushed up, and then think of an angry cat with its back bent in a concave position, head down and tummy tucked in. These two positions are achieved alternatively to efficiently relax your spine, stretch the neck muscles and firm up your glutes.

How-to:

Scan For Audio

1) Assume the mountain posture for about 4 rounds of inhalation and exhalation, with your hands resting on your knees. Now clasp the kneecaps gently with your palms.
2) Get into the cat position by exhaling. Look downwards by drawing your chin towards the neck, draw the stomach in, and round your back to resemble a slouch. Hold this pose for 3 seconds.
3) Proceed to the cow pose while inhaling. Lift your head to the sky, push your chest forward with shoulders rolled backward, and thrust the tailbone out. Keep the buttocks squeezed and hold for a few seconds. Hold the cow position briefly, then go back to the cat position. Keeping the palms on the kneecaps and not letting them slide will help you to better manage this.
4) Repeat steps (2) and (3) alternatively a couple of times or more.

You will find the entire torso and the pelvis relaxing like they have had a body massage. The internal organs also experience stimulation with this gentle treatment.

The Tree Pose 1 (Vrikshasana) #3

This pose will help in appreciating how the body moves during chair yoga. You will notice how, as compared with regular physical exercise regimens, the movements here are slow-paced, extremely mindful, and gentle.

How-to:

Scan For Audio

1) Take the mountain pose with your hands resting at your sides. Now extend the left leg and stretch it as far as you can towards the side. You will find yourself sliding toward the edge of the seat.
2) Bend the knee of the right leg and raise the right heel. Stop to check your balance and bring your hands in front of your chest to the prayer position.

Hold the position for several deep breaths, then get back to an upright position. Repeat on the right side.

Tree Pose 2 (Vrikshasana) #4

How-to:

Scan For Audio

1) Take the mountain pose with your hands resting at your sides. Now gently raise the right leg, and place on the thigh of your left leg.
2) Spread your arms and stretch them straight above the head, clasped together in a prayer position. The act of raising your arms and holding them up for a few seconds helps the lungs to expand, and eases up on the spinal nerves attached to the cord.
3) Stay put for a few seconds and watch your breath. Try to breathe deeply with a more purposeful inhalation and longer exhalation, and take care not to strain. Get back to the mountain pose, and now repeat the tree pose with the left leg. Stay for a similar length of time as with the right leg, then relax.
4) You will feel the diaphragm lifting towards the heart. This is a powerful position that tones the abdomen, pelvis, spine, and upper body.

It results in better balance and toning of the muscles in the legs and hands. Coordinating breathing with body movements will help calm anxiety. You may sometimes notice that the right and left legs have different abilities to sustain the pose. This observation will help one work at overcoming the weaknesses of different parts of your body.

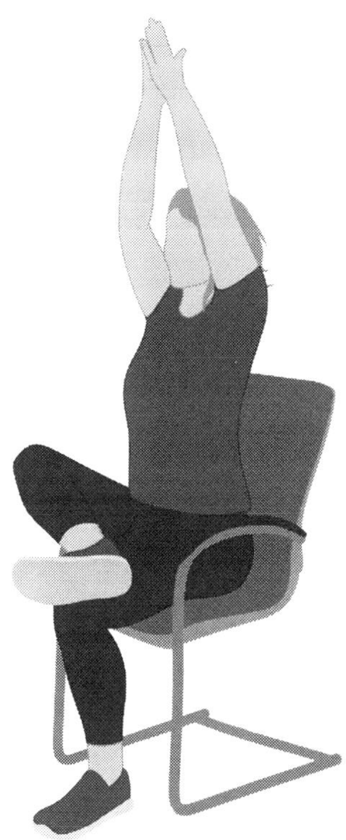

Now that we have experienced a few postures let us take some time to understand another important aspect a bit more closely. The breath according to yoga is something that holds great potential. It is awe-inspiring in the sense that it is an involuntary function like the beating of our hearts and digestion, but also voluntarily malleable, which gives us the power to manipulate the entire nervous system.

CHAPTER 6

The Breathing Blueprint

Breathe. Let go. And remind yourself that this very moment is the only one you know you have for sure.

Oprah Winfrey

An Intrinsic Part of Yoga Practice

When there is an unexpected thing that happens to us, be it stubbing our toe when walking or dealing with a catastrophe, we have a split-second window given to us by the brain to choose our response. We can allow ourselves to be gripped in the spiral of anger, repulsion or fear, or we can take a deep breath to regain control. In extreme emotions, whether positive or negative, we don't always realize that it is the breath that helps us find our bearings. The sages of yore truly captured the connection of breathing with wisdom. The practice of yoga lays a deep emphasis on educating ourselves on the power and potential of the breath.

Mindfulness of breathing or the 'flow of in-breath and out-breath' is an intrinsic part of yoga practice. You will notice that this aspect will be discussed throughout the book at the risk of repetition because it is so crucial. *Pranayama* as it is known in Sanskrit is about gaining control over one's breath. It does not mean you need to strain yourself in the process, it only implies that as a beginner, you will learn to bring your awareness to the process of exhaling and inhaling, and learn to synchronize it with your body movements.

It helps to know that intentional breathing activates the parasympathetic nervous system which kick-starts our brain's relaxation mode and suppresses the sympathetic nervous system that controls the stress response of fight, flight, and freeze.

What to Expect During Breath Training

For starters, drawing attention to your breathing periodically will right away lead to wilful regulation, which in turn will help in controlling the mind in terms of concentration, focus, and channeling of energy. Deep breathing will mean activating the diaphragm to increase the inflow and outflow of air in the respiratory system and decrease the frequency of each cycle.

It regulates the energy flow in the body and helps experience a sense of serenity. It is a fact that a lot of suppressed emotions come out when we start to do breathing exercises. Weeping, rage, cringe, anything society has taught us to suppress will surface during training sessions, and these outbursts in turn resolve issues of anxiety attacks and throw hidden pains out of our systems. Science is backing the claims with growing acknowledgment of the power of breathing. The target of breathwork is thus your mind and not just your lungs.

Breathwork As Against Meditation

Max Strom, the author of A Life Worth Breathing, tells us how popular culture encourages us to numb our feelings that in turn cause stress, burnout and anxiety. Breathing, according to him, is the panacea and he demonstrates how easy-to-practice techniques can make all the difference in helping us regain quality of life.

When we get to the topic of learning to breathe attentively, everyone invariably gets talking about meditation. We would kindly want you to exercise restraint in steering toward the subject at this stage. Meditation is indeed a powerful tool but not at the juncture where we are taking baby steps toward knowing about breathing. Let us begin by being conscious of our breathing and that in itself is a surmountable task.

Elementary Techniques to Start

It Is About Attention and Not Control

Breathing is normally done through the nostrils and never through the mouth unless specified in the asana. Many of us unwittingly use our mouths to breathe and this habit is more common than we think it is. We see this time and again with students expressing surprise at discovering their patterns during training.

Do not try to control your breath rather pay attention to it by following it. When we do this we begin to become more purposeful and the result is deeper inhalations and exhalations. Exhalation or breathing out has to be always twice as long as inhalation or breathing in since it is exhaling that gets the body to relaxing mode. Doing this every time you remember will gradually activate the rest, relaxation, and digestion response of the body, and you will find yourself getting less impulsive or nervous. One can proceed to practice alternate nostril breathing wherein you gently press one nostril with your thumb to allow air to pass in only through one nostril at a time.

Pranayama or Breathing Exercises for Daily Pursuit

We will start breathing practices with a few cautions in mind:

1) Do not try to unnaturally control your breathing if you have not yet received individual guidance for a good period of time. If you are a beginner, follow your natural breathing pattern consciously to achieve deep and deliberate breaths.

2) Forced patterns can aggravate nervous conditions, invite respiratory uneasiness and strain the diaphragm.

Alternate Nostril Breathing (Pranayama) #5

How-to:

Scan For Audio

1) Get to the mountain pose and place your hands on your knees. Take a deep breath, hold it for two seconds and exhale almost twice the length of inhalation. Repeat a few times without straining the breath or chest.
2) Gently press your right thumb on the right nostril to block the airflow and inhale with the left nostril. Exhale through the left nostril and release the thumb. Now do this with the left nostril and repeat the alternations a few times.
3) The next variation is that you inhale with the left nostril and exhale through the left nostril and vice versa. Keep your attention constant on the inflow and outflow of the air and stop if you feel any strain.

Adopt this practice regularly as you sit down to watch television or sit on the park seat during evening outings. Make sure you watch out for any undue strain on the facial muscles and chest while practicing deep exhalation and inhalation. Simple mindful breathing reduces nighttime sleep disturbances since it can increase melatonin levels in the brain and it brings calmness when done in anxiety-causing circumstances.

The Ocean Breath (Ujjayi) #6

How-to:

Scan For Audio

1) Take the mountain pose with the palms facing up. Fold the forefingers to touch the tip of the thumb and maintain this position throughout.
2) Inhale deeply with the mouth kept closed and exhale longer through the mouth with a "Haaaaa" sound. Repeat two to three times.
3) Inhale through the nostrils and this time exhale through the nostrils with the mouth remaining closed and trying to get the "Haaaaa" sound in the throat. You will get the feeling of air escaping through the nostrils and ears as well.

Dr. Andrew Weil's 4-7-8 breath

It is a *pranayama* technique popularized by the Harvard-trained medical practitioner, Dr. Andrew Weil and used by people to get into deep relaxation mode. It entails inhaling to four counts, holding the breath to seven counts, and exhaling to eight counts. It works as an instant remedy during an anxiety-inducing situation and when practiced every day works as a preventive antidote for those who are anxiety prone. The numbers are there to help us get the proportions right and eventually make it a subconscious pattern.

Individual Guidance Is Required for Advanced Practices

At sophisticated levels of Pranayama one gets to master higher yogic practices that are remarkably different from the basic ones and need the guidance of an experienced teacher to avoid any side effects triggered by wrong practices.

To Inhale Or Exhale

It is a great idea to learn to pair up some of the critical movements with their corresponding breath. When we advance to a variety of postures we will want to follow natural breathing tendencies.

You will notice that it seems natural to inhale while lifting your arms up and exhale when bringing them down and therefore becomes the obvious rhythm to follow. Similarly when we bend the body forward and down the torso tightens up and there is a relaxation response stimulated. The natural sequence here would be to exhale. Here it helps to remember not to artificially alter the inhale sequence by any means. Inhaling is the right action when lifting the body up and spreading the shoulders and chest muscles during postures and so is exhaling when turning the body to the left or right.

CHAPTER 7

Getting to Move With the Beginners' Postures

The only way to make progress, the only choice I had, was to start small.

James Clear

See Chair, Think Yoga

We know this, but we forget it, the mind becomes dull and inert when the body is not agile. We then go on to find excuses to justify why the body is not active, 'I am aging and it is natural' being the top one. Reinforcement comes from society too and thus starts the cascading effect on things big and small. Even when one is recovering from a stroke the body is fighting back to reach its optimal state and we owe it to our body to help achieve that. It is not a time-bound achievement and you will be able to perpetually practice it in varying degrees.

The beauty of yoga is that it is process-oriented and not outcome-oriented. The journey itself is the benefit where you are not straining your body for a future result. Hatha Yoga Pradipika, the book speaks on how the young, the frail, the very old, and the sick, can adopt yoga as a companion to wellness provided there is sustained practice. Therefore you see, unlike other exercise systems, fitness is not a prerequisite. The full range of asanas may not be at your disposal but be assured that there is something for everyone. With its mindful and gentle movements that will not stress the joints and muscles, it is an undemanding drill for the body that will benefit anyone who has had a sedentary lifestyle or is diagnosed with age-related illnesses.

Since we are beginning the process of settling the body, mind, and emotions before we can channel our hidden potential, it is totally acceptable to feel bored or worn out occasionally during practice. The solution is to love and discipline yourself as you would a child in your care. We all have our share of stress or trauma on a physical and mental basis. You'll notice a shift in control if you accept them rather than fight them.

Postures for Beginners

The beginner's pose sequence is intended to evaluate your ability to engage the entire body and make sure you are capable of assessing the poses that concentrate on the various muscle groups and joints. After doing the postures described in this chapter, you will be able to tell where your body needs further training. Believe that change will happen with every new attempt.

Shoulder Raise Pose (Urdhva Hastasana) #7

It will help provide elasticity to your shoulders and armpits and ends up sculpting your belly as well. The stretching action of the body enhances digestion too to make it an elegant power-packed drill. Begin with one arm and proceed to use both arms together.

How-to:

Scan For Audio

1) Take the mountain position well, inhale and raise your arms in a slow and deliberate movement to the chest level with palms facing each other and now continue the movement until the fingers point upwards. Take care to always keep them parallel to each other with the biceps closer to the ears.
2) Allow the hands to extend upwards as much as your shoulders allow you. Keep the fingertips stretched. If your shoulders allow, try and bring the palms together or else take them slightly apart so that you are able to hold the position for a few seconds.
3) Feel the chest muscles opening up and the rib cage expanding. Keep your naval tucked in and raise the chin to a forward glance.
4) Hold the position and your breath for a few seconds. Take your attention to the legs to make sure the toes are flat on the ground. Exhale long and gently get back to the upright position by bringing the hands down by your sides and placing the palms back on the knees.

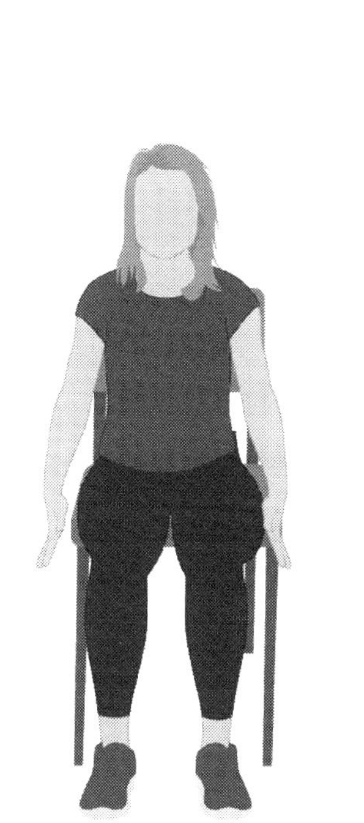

Modification

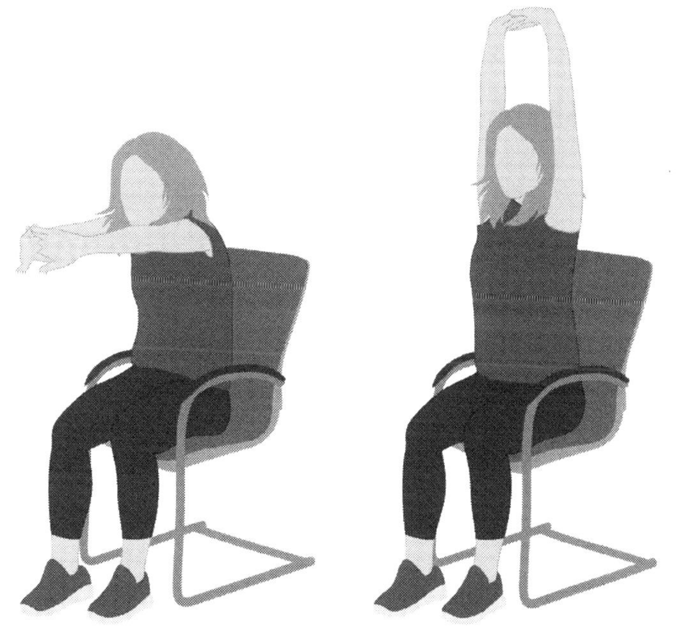

Reverse Prayer Pose (Paschima Namaskarana) #8

How-to:

Scan For Audio

1) Sit in an upright position. Keep your eyes closed and take deep uniform breaths. Feel the diaphragm rise and fall with each cycle. Keep bringing your attention back to the body if your thoughts are straying by default as they tend to.
2) Raise your hands gently and bring them behind you to rest on your lower spine. Turn the wrists and try to bring the palms together to the praying position, if not clasp them together at ease.
3) Continue breathing and feel your chest expanding and collar bones stretching. Tuck the tummy in and push the tailbone out to achieve a good posture.
4) Now pull your head backward to look up at the ceiling or sky, bring them back to position, and bend downwards towards the chest. Bring it back to an upright position, and turn your neck to the right and then to the left. You are welcome to repeat the neck exercises to help soothe your cervical nodes.

Camel Posture (Ustrasana) #9

How-to:

Scan For Audio

1) Sit back well into the chair, inhale and arch your shoulders and head backward so that they rest on top of the backrest.
2) Lift your chin up and pay attention to the collar bones and hip joints to ensure they are all aligned comfortably.
3) Let your arms fall easily on the sides of the chair. The palms need to face forwards and the elbows stretched straight.
4) Stay in the position and inhale deeply so that the chest pushes forward and the spinal cord curves well. Continue to take more rounds of breaths and feel the sensations on the collar bones and spine.

This posture loosens up the vertebrae increasing blood circulation in the spinal column and also aids in digestion due to the expansion of the abdominal region.

Reclining Pigeon Pose (Supta Kapotasana) #10

This is a delightful pose that will surely make you want to practice every day. It engages the hamstrings and opens up stiff hip bones efficiently.

How-to:

Scan For Audio

1) Sit in an upright position (you know by now). Take care to keep the spine stretched up to sit tall.
2) Inhale, and gently lift the right leg by supporting the hamstring muscles by clasping it with one or both hands if you have to. Bring the right foot to rest on the left thigh by pulling the feet gently with one hand.
3) Adjust the angle to your comfort. It is okay if the ankle doesn't yield just yet as it will get better with warm-ups. Support the right knee by placing your right hand underneath if you have to.
4) Exhale and gently bend forward without letting the shoulders droop while holding the position for about 5 counts. Keep the heels of the left leg firm on the ground. You feel the hips stretching and the hamstrings expanding. Bring your attention to it and hold your position.
5) Hold for at least 5 counts, inhale, make sure the upper body does not wobble, straighten up and exhale and release the right leg to reestablish the upright posture. Repeat on the left side.

Please make sure you don't currently have a hip injury or have recently undergone hip surgery because this position extends the hip joints.

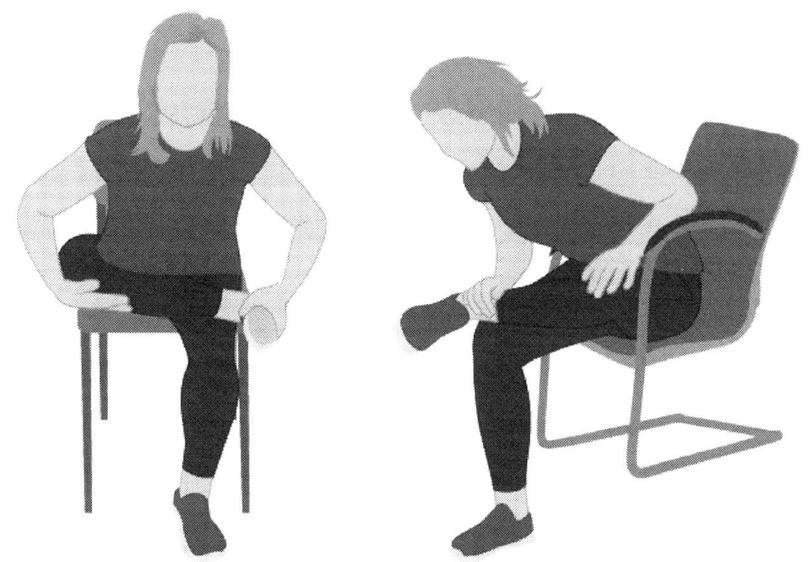

Bound Angle Pose (Baddha Konasana) #11

This is a pose where you will keep the knees apart and bring the heels together to help rotate the hip joints and loosen up the thigh muscles.

How-to:

Scan For Audio

1) Sit upright with your glutes resting on the front end of the chair with your palms kept on the thighs.
2) Spread the thighs outwards till the knees face outwards in the opposite directions.
3) As you spread the thighs bring the heels together to touch and gently lift them off the ground, with the toes facing outwards like the knees.
4) Check your posture and hold the position to at least 10 counts with attention on the breath as well. It is okay not to be able to hold long initially. It will get better.
5) Maintain the thighs apart by using your palms to nudge them outward.

The Seated Twist (Bharadvajasana) #12

How-to:

Scan For Audio

1) Take the mountain pose, but this time seated facing the left side of your chair. The backrest will be across your left shoulder. Slide towards the front end of the chair and open up the palms as they face frontward, and pull the arms to a firm stretch.
2) Inhale while checking your posture, and exhale while turning your torso to the left. Make sure your glutes don't shift and the movement is only waist upwards. Hold for a while to check for drooping shoulders and hold the backrest with both hands.
3) Your gaze has to be straight ahead of the backrest and also make sure that the knees are close to each other. Hold the position to feel the sensations.
4) Inhale and bring the body back to the upright position. Exhale and raise your arms by the sides of the ears. Inhale and get back to the mountain position.
5) Shift to the right side to repeat on the other side. Keep practicing to make the right and left twists equally comfortable if you notice any discrepancies.

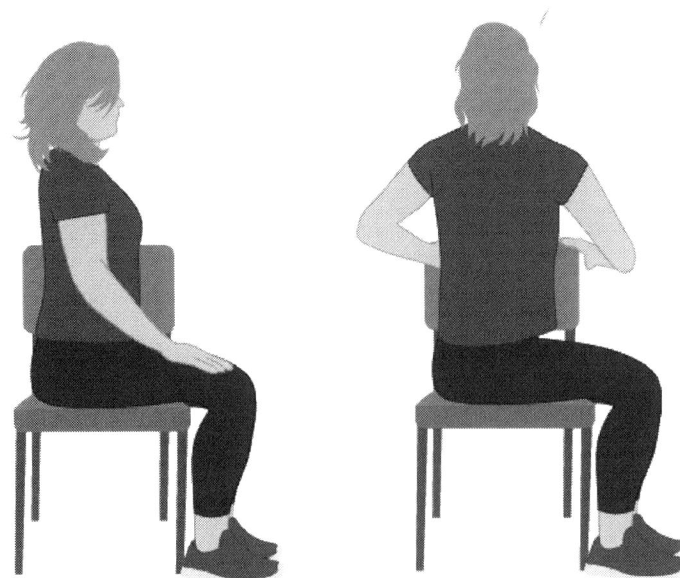

Modification

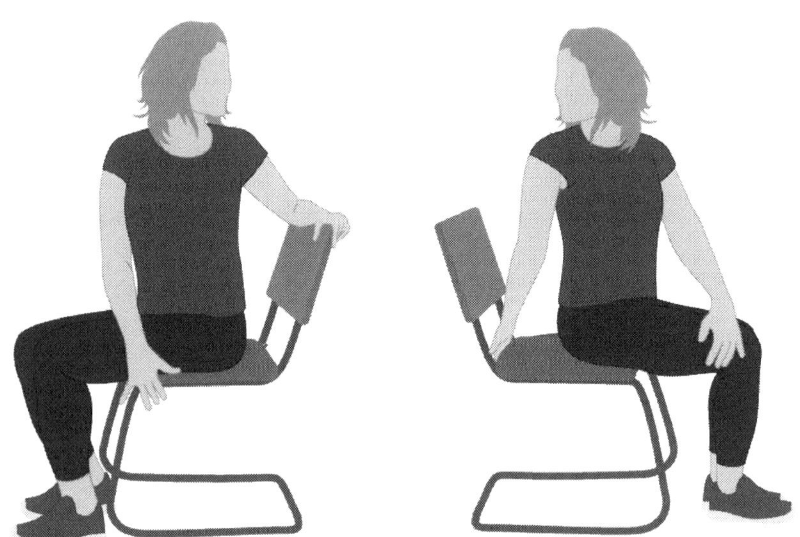

Seated Low Lunge (Anjaneyasana) #13

How-to:

Scan For Audio

1) From the mountain position gently lift the right leg to have the foot in front of the chair seat. Hold the position by supporting the thigh with the hands.
2) The back should remain in an upright position without resting on the backrest of the chair.
3) Press the clasped palms to bring the thigh to the chest. If it does not quite reach you can stop where there is resistance. Do not force but breathe and bring your attention to the sensation.
4) Place your right foot back on the ground and repeat with the left leg. Practice this to open up your hamstrings and hips and strengthen the pelvic floor muscles.

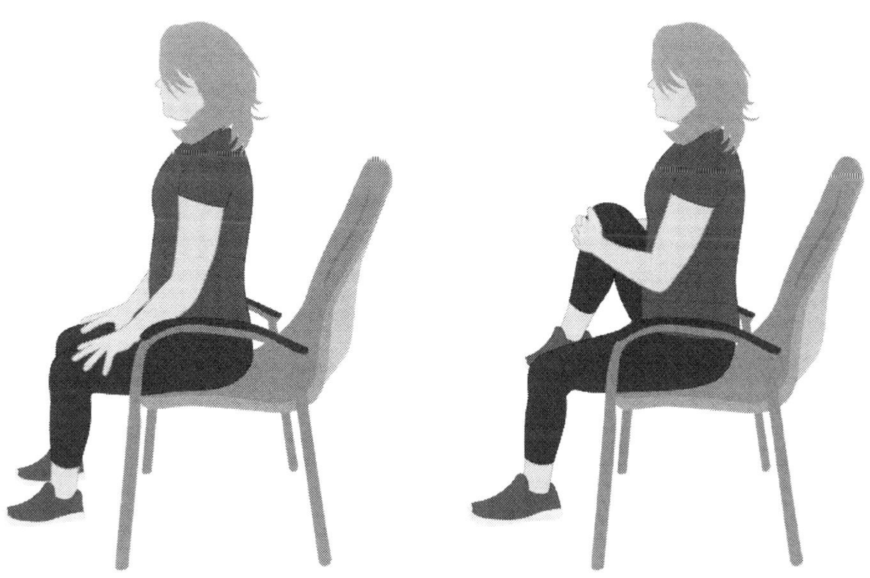

The Cobra Pose (Bhujangasana) #14

The cobra pose helps to squeeze the back for a self-massage and open up the chest and shoulder muscles. Below are instructions of how to perform the cobra pose seated however, this pose is commonly achieved by lying on the floor belly down and lifting the upper body to achieve a grace curve like a snake with its hood up in all glory.

How-to:

Scan For Audio

1) Sit up straight towards the outer edge with the feet placed rather close to each other. Place your palms on either side of your buttocks holding the edges of the chair.
2) Inhale deeply and gently thrust the torso forward looking up to the sky as you move forward. Push down the palms into the seat for support.
3) Feel the navel tuck in, your tailbone pushes outward, chest muscles expand, your shoulders spread and the shoulder blades lean into the spinal cord as you expand forward. Hold this position and get back to an upright position as you exhale long and strong. Repeat a few times.

Child's Pose (Balasana) #15

The child's pose provides relief to chronic back pains and is ideal for someone confined to a wheelchair or with limited mobility. Depending on the health condition one must feel free to use blocks to raise the legs up or use a chair placed in front with cushions to provide support for bending. It encourages one to stretch the spine to provide the decompression that is needed to combat the ill effects of prolonged sitting.

We love this pose because it allows many of us to try it on the bed just as we wake up. Sitting upright with legs tucked under the buttocks, bend forward onto the bed and hold a few moments to find yourself instantly refreshed.

Props Required for Variations: Blocks to Raise the Legs/One More Chair

How-to:

Scan For Audio

1) Sit deep into the chair and place your hands on the knees with the legs apart hip wide. Keep your spine straight and sit tall as if to push the head gently up.
2) Taking care not to slouch, slowly start bending forward. Observe the body sensations keenly as you progress. If you feel resistance in the spine, hip or neck stop right there and take a deep breath. Progress if the body allows or else get back to an upright position and repeat after a few warm-ups.
3) Allow the hands to stretch straight ahead as you bend to rest your chest on the thighs. Keep the spine straight as if to push an imaginary object forward with your head. This ensures that you achieve as much spine extension as possible. You can lower your hands and allow them to hang by the sides, let them touch the ground, or even cross them under your thighs to sustain the position for a longer time.

4) It is a good idea to use blocks under the legs to raise the knees. Place the blocks at step (1) if you plan to use them. This will help in achieving the body bend for someone with chronic back pain.
5) Placing another chair facing you about a foot in front will help support the hands to sustain a longer duration.
6) This pose is extremely relaxing and provides instant relief to stiff bones. Relax and get back to an upright position.

CHAPTER 8

Active-Seated Postures for Toning up the Body

People often say that motivation doesn't last. Well, neither does bathing- that's why we recommend it daily.

Zig Ziglar

In yoga, the body is never pushed against its natural resistance. The elasticity and flexibility needed are attained through extremely gentle and consistent stretches. A poor posture can affect gait and balance and also your breathing patterns. It helps to keep in mind that every time we stretch to an unfamiliar pose we will hold the position and breathe deeply. Breathing brings awareness to the limitations of the body and at the same time its potential. We learn the subtle art of listening to our body and mind. The sequence of exercises explained here can be done one following the other. If you want to do just a bunch of them at a time you are welcome to do so.

The Toe Raise and Curl Warm Up #16

How-to:

Scan For Audio

1) Take the mountain position with the mind, body, and spirit. Hold a few moments and move your glutes a little toward the front edge of the seat.
2) With the heels and the metatarsals firmly rooted to the ground start tapping the floor with the toes. Begin with slow counts as this can be quite a deal if you are not used to moving the toes.
3) A few counts later lift the metatarsals and curl your toes. Curl and release a few counts. Stop and relax.

Do not get carried away and overdo it since the toes and calf muscles can hurt the next day if strained.

Toe Point and Flex Warm Up #17

How-To:

Scan For Audio

1) This pose can be performed seated on a chair or sitting on the floor. If performed seated on a chair it will required greater leg strength. Inhale gently and lift both legs to get them parallel to the floor with your toes pointing away from you.
2) Exhale and flex the ankles to get your toes pointing to the sky. Inhale and push the toes away from you. Repeat gently while taking care to keep your legs parallel to the ground constantly.

If you mobility permits, you may find it less strenuous to perform this pose sitting on the floor, or propped up in bed with your back resting against the headboard.

Running Warm-up #18

How-to:

Scan For Audio

1) Sit back in the chair with your shoulder blades leaning on the backrest.
2) Hold the sides of the chair and lift the knees alternatively to push the feet back to imitate the running action.
3) The torso should lean forwards to provide balance to the body.
4) Control the speed of movement to ensure that the kneecaps do not strain.
5) Continue for about 20 counts.

This fast-paced yet controlled action will get your legs active and heart beat high to get some calories burning.

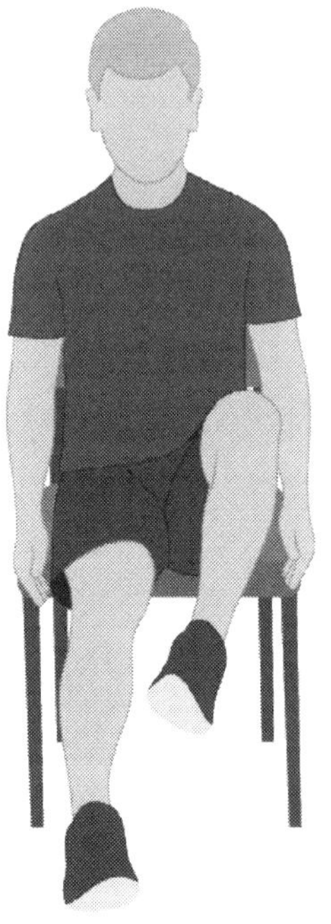
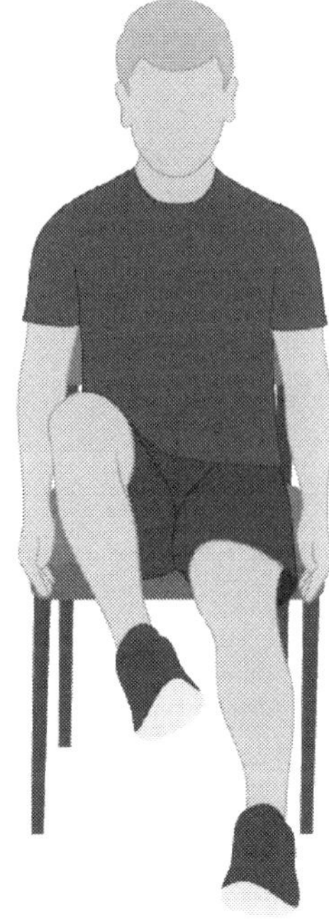

Side Sprawl Pose (Utthita Parsvakonasana) #19

How to:

Scan For Audio

1) Sit upright in the mountain pose with palms facing up. Bring the buttocks forward towards the front edge of the chair.
2) Spread the legs sideways to the sides of the chair with the knees bent and facing outwards, and slowly extend the right leg.
3) Raise your right arm to shoulder height and hold for a while. Bend towards the left side with the left forearm resting on the thigh.
4) Now bring the right hand over the head and stretch. Gaze up and observe the right palm, and hold the position for 5 counts.
5) Release the position and return to the upright position to be ready to repeat on the right.

This posture will help relax the pelvic region and prevent stiff backs that commonly occur with age or a sedentary lifestyle.

The Warrior Pose 1 (Virabhadrasana 1) #20

How-to:

Scan For Audio

1) Sit upright in a mountain pose pushing yourself to the front edge of the chair.
2) Spread your feet apart to get the thighs in a v-shape. Gently straighten out the right leg with the toes facing outwards. Now turn at the waist to face the left side. If you were facing north in an upright position, you would now be looking west. The buttocks will slightly dislodge from the seat and shift to the right. You will observe your left foot turning naturally. Bring it to a 90-degree turn and keep the leg vertical to the ground. The right foot would have turned slightly right.
3) Stretch out the right leg. Raise your hands to a prayer position above the head and turn your gaze to the palms overhead. That's your perfect pose. However, we will not aim at achieving this posture on the first try. Observe your body at each movement and stop when there is resistance. You would like to place one hand on the backrest and that is just as fine. Hold for about 5 seconds while breathing evenly.

   Get back to mountain pose with hands down by the side at the stage you feel stretched. Relax and repeat.
4) Repeat on the left side just the same.

The Warrior Pose 2 (Virabhadrasana 2)

How-to:

Scan For Audio

1) Sit in a mountain posture towards the edge of the chair. Inhale and spread your arms sideways at shoulder level, palms facing the floor. Spread the feet apart with knees straight to the fullest extent possible.
2) Turn right from the waist upwards and align the right leg with the toes facing right and the shin at 90 degrees to the ground. Keep the left leg straight with the knees firmed up. Keep your arms fully spread out and straight.
3) Stay put till you are stable and return to the upright position.

Repeat all the steps to achieve the same posture on the left side.

You will find your muscles becoming more elastic with each round of yoga postures and observe a spring in your mind as well.

Seated Boat Pose (Navasana) #21

How-to:

Scan For Audio

1) Sit upright and gently lift your legs. You can use your hands under the thighs to prop them up. See if you can hold them up to have the shin parallel to the ground.
2) Release the hands and straighten them forward parallel to the ground.
3) Maintain the posture with the navel tucked in and stay a few breaths. Slowly move back to the starting position.

Finding your balance can be difficult in the beginning but is sure to improve with practice. If you find raise both legs initially challenging, start by raise one leg, pause for a few breaths before slowly lowering it and repeating the movement with the other leg. As your balance and confidence improve progress to raising both legs.

Modification

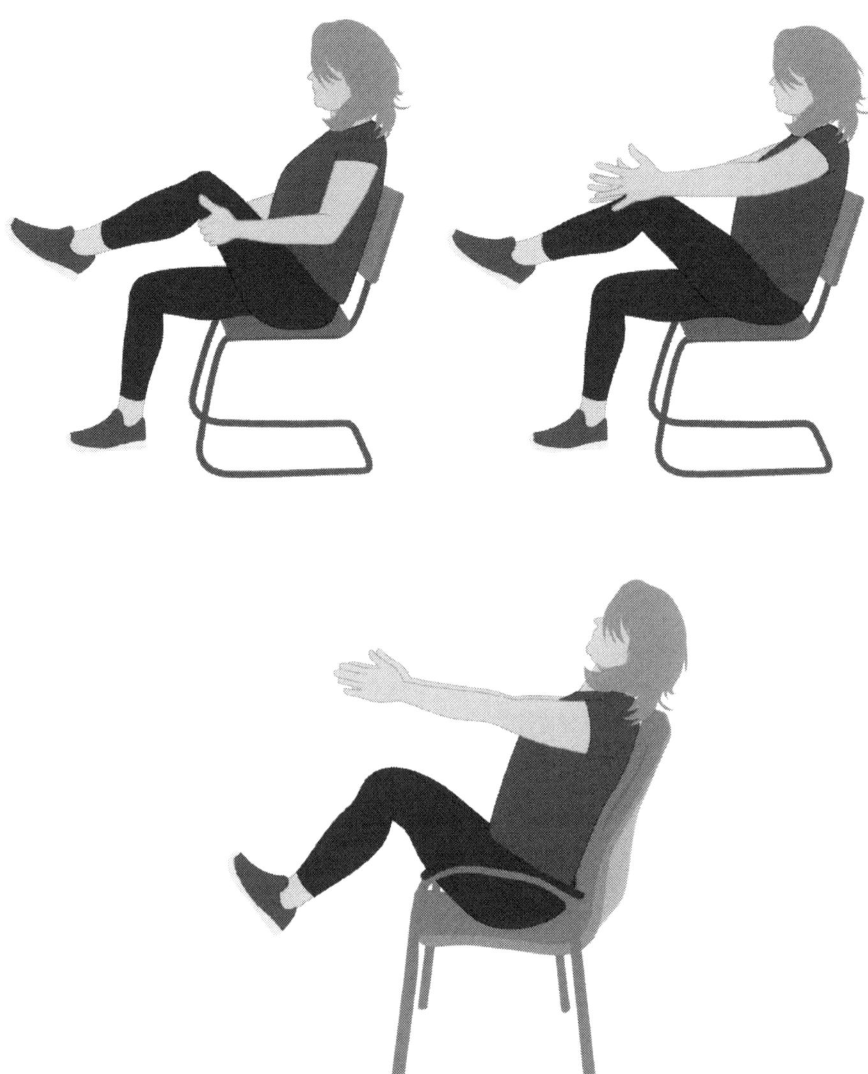

Seated Butterfly Pose (Baddha Konasana) #22

This is an effective pelvic strengthening exercise and is highly recommended for addressing lower back issues. It opens up the hip and calms the mind therefore is an antidote to hours of sitting in one position.

How-to:

Scan For Audio

1) To start with a half-butterfly pose you will take the mountain posture with your hands on your knees.
2) Using your right hand gently lift the right foot and place it on the chair seat. The sole should touch the inner thighs of the left leg. Stabilize your body in this posture with the back straight and shoulders spread out.
3) With the hand continuing to grasp the feet begin to flap the right leg up and down like a butterfly. Achieve about ten gentle flaps and place the leg down. Repeat with the left leg.
4) Now with some confidence try to lift both legs simultaneously to the seat. Keep the soles pressed against each other while holding them with your hands and flap both legs simultaneously. Remember to keep the back straight by bringing your awareness back to it periodically.

CHAPTER 9

Yoga for Your Neck, Shoulders, and Arms

My actions are my only true belongings.

Thich Nhat Hanh

Yoga for Hands and Fingers

When you aren't able to open the cookie jar with ease, do you feel like things are literally getting out of hand? Being unable to move our hands freely due to rigidity is really annoying. When we turn that doorknob or pick up our cup of coffee, we notice how rheumatoid and other types of arthritis limit our hands' range of motion.

While arthritis and dislocations need medical attention, the asanas will act as an efficient complement. Taking a few moments every day to tend to our hands will present significant relief since we sometimes tend to give up on exercises due to discomfort felt after the first few sessions. It is important to sustain and the answer to it is to do your daily workout to keep the movement alive.

The here-explained exercises are great for loosening up stiff hands and fingers. We must keep in mind that yoga is based on the notion of totality and does not operate independently on certain parts only. By remembering that the entire body, the intellect, and the spirit are equally involved when we work on the fingers, we are able to achieve our goals. We won't miss our posture patterns, mood, or the reality that we are a part of everything around us when we keep our attention on our fingers.

Mudras For Fingers

Yoga has a sophisticated group of movements designed for the hands called *mudras*. *Mudra* means gesture and is a subtle movement that is in itself a large body of work that aims at channelling the energy of the body. It works on influencing our moods, attitude, and perception. As always the objective of *mudras* is not just physical fitness. We will use some of the very basic mudras to build agility in the fingers.

How-to:

Scan For Audio

1) Sit in an upright position and join your palms in front of your chest. This is the Anjali mudra or the praying pose. Inhale and lift the arms to bring the elbows to the level of the face. Exhale and bring the clasped palms back to the chest position and repeat.
2) Keep the praying hands in front of the chest and gently pull the lower palms apart while keeping the fingertips touching to form a dome. Press back the palms and repeat while incorporating the breathing as you close and open the palms. Rest your hands back on your knees.
3) Lift your hands with palms facing up and bring the index finger to the tip of the thumb to form a circle with them. Spread the other fingers straight and apart. Place the back of the palms on the knees. Inhale deeply and exhale long a few times.
4) Lift your hands, extend them, turn the palms outwards at chest level, sit tall and bend each of the fingers separately to touch the root of the thumb. Hold it pressed gently with the thumb each time. Take time to inhale and exhale with each flexed finger to feel calm.
5) Get the hands back to the praying position and spread the fingers wide. Cross over the fingers into the webs of the hands and press gently to feel the fingers being massaged. Fold and clasp the hands. Inhale, exhale and relax with hands back on the knees.

Star Fish Spread

How-to:

Scan For Audio

1) Take the mountain pose with your hands on your knees. Take your time to inhale and exhale and feel the body.
2) Lift both hands to your front at chest level, palms downward, inhale and spread the fingers wide like a starfish.
3) Extend the arms forward and keep the shoulders pulled back to achieve full expansion of the arm. Notice the sensation in the fingers.
4) One hand at a time, turn the palms upwards and downwards without allowing the shoulders to droop. Inhale and exhale gently as you change the direction of the palms. You will feel the gentle pull in the forearms as you move your wrists.
5) Get back the hands to rest on the knees and relax. Draw attention to the warming up of the fingers, knuckles, wrists, and arms.

Upside-down Starfish Spread

How-to:

Scan For Audio

1) Raise the hands forward again and follow steps (1) and (2).
2) Raise your palms at the wrist so that the fingers point to the sky. Keep them upright like you would push an imaginary object. Engage the lower part of the palm as well. Hold, inhale and exhale a few times.
3) Keep the fingers spread, inhale and turn the left wrist clockwise and right wrist anti-clockwise simultaneously to let the fingers point towards each other. Again push an imaginary wall with the palms to engage the muscles.
4) Exhale and bring them back up. When you feel the tension in the palms allow them to droop down. Rest your hands on your knees and relax.

It is better to step up the repetitions gradually since the hand muscles take their time to adapt to stretching up. Give your fingers a gentle massage for all the hard work.

Upside-Down Finger Extensions

How-to:

Scan For Audio

1) Follow steps (1), (2) and (3) of the starfish spread to get the palms outward fingers facing the floor.
2) Keeping the right hand in position, use the left hand to gently pull back one at a time all the fingers of the right hand. Start with the little finger and pull it gently towards your chest and proceed with the rest of the fingers.
3) Keep the movements slow, inhale deeply and exhale as long as you attend lovingly to each of the digits. This one provides relief to stiff knuckles. We will remember to correct our posture by not letting the shoulders droop.

Yoga for Neck and Arm Strength

We were not exactly surprised that Cathy was not able to keep her arms raised for even a couple of seconds. She said the last time she remembers the need to keep her arms raised was sixty-five years ago when her nursery teacher told her off for talking incessantly in class. Our present-day lifestyle does not demand a lot with regard to the range of motion of our bodies and as we age we face the consequences. When we don't use it, we lose it! We notice that we are susceptible to injuries or fractures with every slip and trip. Here are some effective postures to practice for flexible and strong arms and guess what, reduce a hunchback.

Goddess Arm Pose (Utkata Konasana) #24

The pose conveys power and grace and lifts up your mood in an instant.

How-to:

Scan For Audio

1) Bring yourself towards the front edge of the seat and spread the legs at the thighs as wide as you can. The thighs will spread to the side of the chair helping you place the legs on either side of the chair with the metatarsals and heels firm on the ground. The toes should point outwards at all times.
2) The chair seat will help you maintain the spread to help relax the hamstrings. Raise both your hands on the side to get the palms by the side of and level with the ears. Keep the palms facing forward and spread the fingers that are pointing upwards. Lift the chin up and look straight ahead with a feeling of elegance. This is the goddess position.
3) Keep the spine straight, pull in the stomach. The shoulders will be rolled back with shoulder blades leaning towards the spine. Maintain the posture by bringing your attention periodically to the shoulders and spine and take care to distribute the body weight equally on both legs.
4) Once you achieve the goddess position take the time to feel the power of the pose. Inhale and exhale for a few moments. Exhale and bring the forearms together in front of your face. Do not let the biceps droop down or the pelvic muscles cave in.
5) Inhale and gently raise your hands, hold, exhale and get the hands back to the goddess position. Repeat about 6 times.
6) Add in a variation by bending on the sides in the goddess position. Keep your hands stable, inhale and bend to the left. Exhale and get back. Inhale and bend to the right. Exhale and get back to position.

Practicing cactus arms help open up the chest muscles and consequently improves the breathing pattern that gets restricted when the rib cage goes tight with tendencies to sit all hunched up.

7) Goddess Pose Twist: Get to the goddess position, inhale, and turn to the right as far as your waist allows you. Exhale and hold the pose without letting the hands droop. You will feel the right shoulder blade pushing in. Feel the sensation and breath. Inhale and get back to position. Repeat on the left side.

8) Goddess Arm Raise: Get to the goddess position, breathe in, and simultaneously raise your glutes up from the seat to bring the torso up. Maintain the position of the hands by your sides and use the chair to maintain balance by keeping the thighs touching the sides of the chair. Exhale and sit back. Begin with 1 or 2 raises before you feel the confidence to move on to more.

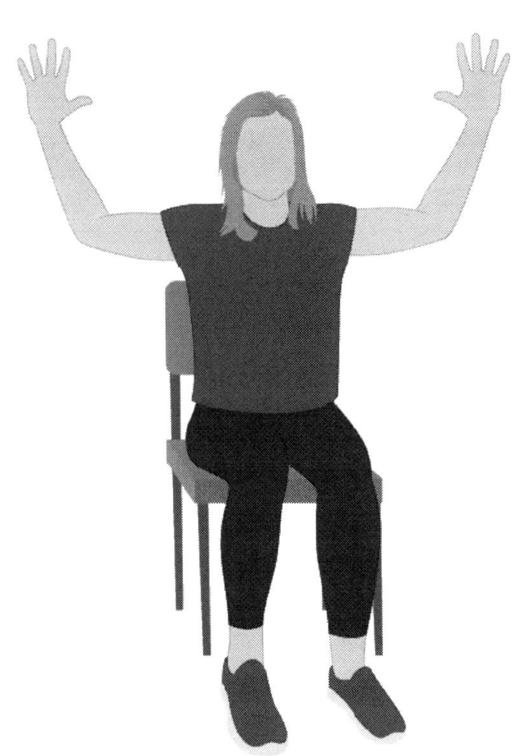

Bow and Arrow Pose (Akarna Dhanurasana) #25

It is helpful as a therapeutic asana for cervical spondylitis and neck or shoulder stiffness.

How-to:

Scan For Audio

1) In the upright position raise your right arm towards the front at a 45-degree angle as if to hold up a bow with the palm clenched. The arm should be placed in front of the corner of the right eye and above eye level.
2) Raise your left arm with palms clenched and bring it towards the right arm such that both arms are towards the side of your body and parallel to each other.
3) Do a pulling action with the left arm as if you are shooting an arrow and bring it back to have both arms stretched.
4) Inhale as you pull back and exhale as you get your hand back and repeat the push-pull action a few times. Get back to the upright position and repeat on the left side.

Yoga for Your Wrists and Elbows

Our tendency to use one arm over the other contributes to the misalignment of the strength of the muscles. Yoga is a great way to bring our attention and practice mindful utilization of our arms when medical conditions reported by friends alert us to look for a healthy routine targeting the arms.

A medical diagnosis like tennis elbow is ascertained when we go to our doctor having noticed sharp pains along the forearm. It would have started with a vague pain in the elbows and forearms when doing mundane things like lifting a book, chopping an onion, or even shaking hands at a get-together. Yoga movements done under expert advice can be your perfect complement to medical treatment. It is pertinent to avoid wrong exercises that can lead to undue straining and stretching and hence we must check on the ones to be avoided altogether. The poses mentioned below were chosen to avoid weight on the wrists and arms.

Wrist Extension And Rotation Warm-Up

How-to:

Scan For Audio

1) Sit lovingly in an upright position and tend to your wrists. It deserves the nourishment and care to get it going. Bring your palms together at chest level in a deliberate way with full awareness of the physicality of your hands.
2) Bring them close to your chest in a praying position with the back straight, shoulders spread, and elbows lifted. Inhale deep, exhale longer and bring your attention to the palm muscles touching each other. There can be discomfort in the forearms and biceps if one is not used to keeping the hands this way. Nothing to worry about and conscious pursuit will take care of any resistance.
3) Unclasp and stretch your arms to the front with palms facing down. Inhale and lift the palms to point your fingertips to the ceiling to give the wrists a little stretch.
4) Hold for 5 counts, exhale and allow the palms to rest back. Repeat.
5) Back extension: Swing your arms to the back of the chairs from the sides. Spread the chests wide and stretch the arms with palms facing outwards.
6) Lift the fingers to flex the wrists. Hold a few moments and bring the hands back on the knees.
7) With the left hand give a gentle massage to the right wrist by gently pressing them, noticing the aches or tenderness if any, and repeat for the right arm.
8) Side extension: Now stretch your hands towards the sides of the chair at seat level, spread the fingers, and press the wrists with fingertips angling up as if to press down an imaginary object. Hold a few moments and relax. Repeat a few times.

9) Bring your hands back in front of your chest and clench the fingers together. Push the arms straight forward and gently begin rotating the wrists in outward circles a few times and then in inward circles. We will now add a variation by spreading the fingers as you rotate the wrists as if to grab the air around as the fingers move in a circle. Relax.
10) Once you are regular with the wrist extension and rotations it will be easy to move on to the Cross Arm Eagle Hand Pose and Hands Under Legs Pose to improve the tenacity of the wrists.

Elbow Turn Warm-up

Arm movements achieved with the help of a pillow on your lap are a splendid idea to support the forearms.

How-to:

Scan For Audio

1) Place a soft pillow on your lap and sit in an upright position with the forearms resting on the pillow. Move the fingers in a wave and move the wrists up down and inward outward to warm up the muscles and joints.
2) Straighten the hands with palms facing downward. The hands need to be placed outside the pillow with the forearms resting on it. Inhale and gently turn the right palm facing up. Feel the sensation at the right elbow. Exhale and turn the palm back. Repeat a few times.
3) Repeat with the left arm and now simultaneously turn the right and left palms to alternate the upwards and downward positions.

Elbow Press Warm-up

How-to:

Scan For Audio

1) Sit in the mountain posture and raise your arms to place both your palms at the back of the head. Clasp the palms for better support. Check your posture, inhale and gently bring the elbows together to meet in front of the face at eye level. Exhale and spread the arms back.
2) Hold with palms continuing to clasp each other and feel the sensations of the arm muscles and shoulder blades. You would not be able to get the elbows to touch each other immediately. Repeat and notice the gradual improvement in flexibility.

Cross Arm Eagle Hand (Garudasana) #26

How-to:

Scan For Audio

1) Raise your right hand and cross it over the chest to the left side. You can grasp the shoulder for better support and hold the position to determine the flexibility of the right shoulder bone.
2) Lift your left arm and cross it over to the right side from under the right elbow. Grasp the right upper arm and squeeze gently. Hold for about five seconds and release. Repeat on the left side.
3) After a few rounds raise both your arms to chest level, and bend at the elbows so that you face your open palms. Keep them straight so that the upper arms are raised at chest level and your palms are above eye level. This is important for you to be able to cross your arms at the elbow.
4) Now cross the left hand in front of the right hand and lock the right elbow with the left. You will feel the right shoulder getting a gentle tug. Hold a few moments to repeat on the right.

This helps in relaxing the upper back and biceps and keeps the wrists and elbows active to alleviate symptoms of arthritis.

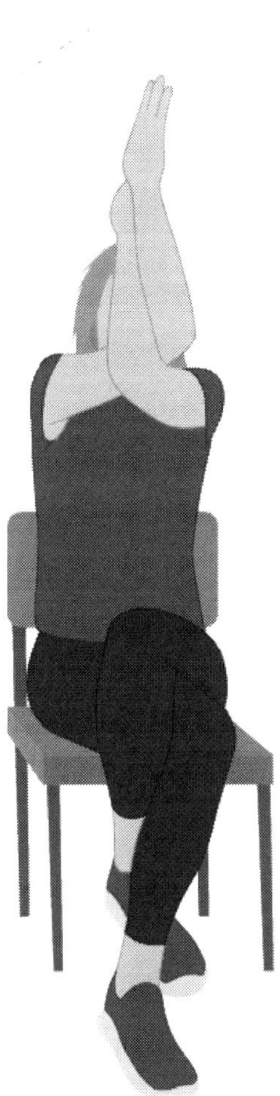

The Cow Face Pose (Gomukhasana) #27

How-to:

Scan For Audio

Prop needed: A full-sized hand towel or yoga straps

1) In the upright position, hold one side of the hand towel with your left hand and flip it on your back to let it run along the spinal cord.
2) Bend your right arm across your waist to grab the other end of the towel at the back. You will now have the towel firmly held vertically and parallel to the spine. We will ensure that it is held at the nape and waist with both hands thus engaging the elbows to provide an extension. Once you have obtained the upright position with the towel behind you, hold the position and breathe.
3) To transfer the towel to the right arm, release the towel from your left hand at the nape and bring the towel to the front with your right arm from across the waist. Flip the towel over the right shoulder to repeat on the right.
4) Sit back upright with the towel resting on the lap. Clasp the towel with both hands, lift it to chest level, and wring the towel both ways as if to squeeze out water. Along with the wrists, you will notice the tension in the elbows. Repeat and relax.
5) Fold the towel to resemble a log of wood and place it on the lap. Inhale and with both hands grasp the towel towards the ends with your palms facing up and lift with elbows bent inwards to rest the towel on your chest. Pull the towel gently apart to keep it stretched throughout. Exhale, stretch the elbows and extend the arms outwards to bring the towel at arm's length from your body. Repeat.

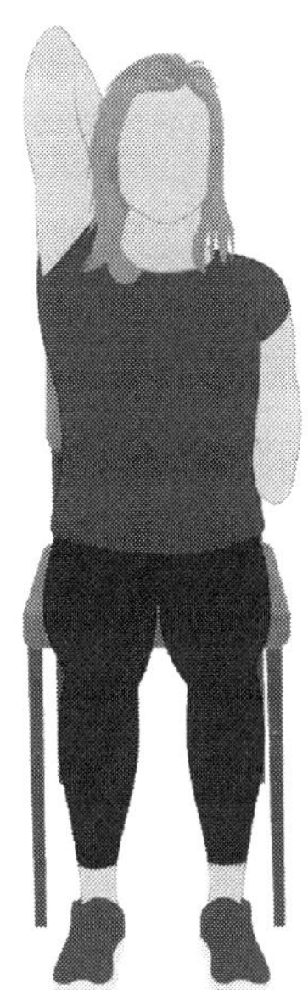

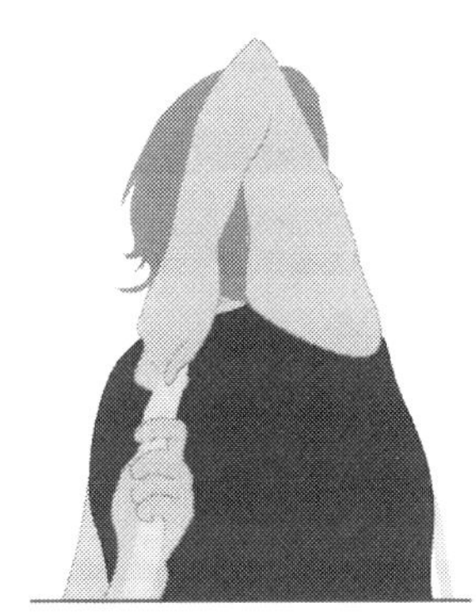

Modification

Yoga for Shoulder Strength

Shoulder Rotations: Three Variations Warm-up

How-to:

Scan For Audio

1) Sit in an upright position taking care not to rest your body on the chair. Inhale and bring your hand to your shoulders to clasp them at the joints with all the fingers and the thumb. Exhale and push the elbows down and up like a bird in flight. Inhale while raising it and exhale when going down and repeat a few times over.
2) Exhale and roll the elbows towards each other so that they touch in front of the chest. Bring them up to face level, inhale and roll to spread them back to their original position. You would have drawn two imaginary circles with the elbows. Repeat.
3) Clench your hands as if to hold two oars and make a rowing a boat movement with both arms simultaneously. This helps in opening the shoulders and working the biceps. Take care not to slouch and keep the tummy tucked in as you row in gentle motions.
4) Rest the hands on the knees for a few movements to observe the sensations.
5) We will now do a movement that calls for using one arm at a time. Sit upright with hands on the knees. Inhale and raise the right arm.
6) Exhale, and take a bow to let the right arm swing down. Continue the swing backward and let it stretch back well, inhale and get back to position sitting tall and with the hands up. You will see that the arms have gone a full circle by sweeping the floor. Repeat on the left side.

Shoulder Roll Warm-Up

How-to:

Scan For Audio

1) Sit in an upright position with your hands on the knees. Inhale and gently shrug your shoulders to bring them towards the ears. Exhale and let the shoulder joints roll forward and downward while gradually releasing the shrug.
2) Shrug again and this time roll the shoulder joints backward and down to release the shrug. Hold and feel the sensations of the neck and shoulder muscles.

Shoulder rolls must precede other shoulder exercises to reduce symptoms of arthritis and osteoporosis, and it helps bring your attention to any discomfort in movement that you would like to report to your doctor.

CHAPTER 10

Seated Postures That Will Vitalize Your Core and Lower Back

Flexibility makes buildings to be stronger, imagine what it can do to your soul.

Carlos Barrios

We will need to admit that sitting upright with the body weight distributed well onto the legs, hips, and pelvis does not come naturally or is even expected of us in our daily life. We do not think twice before leaning on the backrest of our chairs a few seconds into sitting or shopping for cushioned couches to sink into. These habits built over decades have a direct bearing on core strength as age advances.

By practicing chair yoga, we challenge ourselves to change from one subtle position to the next. Consider now what that implies to us. When we intentionally shift our bodies, we gain a greater understanding of how they behave and are far better able to coordinate our movements. Our proprioception develops and this plays a significant role in preventing falls and sprains.

Five Pointed Star Warm-up #28

How-to:

Scan For Audio

1) Sit well on the front edge of the chair so that the legs can move freely to the sides.
2) Inhale and spread your arms at shoulder level and sideways. Keep the fingers spread wide.
3) Simultaneously stretch the legs sideways to match the spread of the arms. Remember to keep the spine straight to keep the posture intact. Hold and count to 4.
4) Exhale and pull back the arms and legs to regain the upright position. Repeat a few times to get the coordination right.

This warm up is good for lengthening and aligning the spine, hip joints and shoulders.

Easy Pose (Sukhasana) #29

The name is deceptive, be warned. It is going to test your core strength, but don't worry, it is equally benevolent.

How-to:

Scan For Audio

1) Take an upright position with the spine stretched up and the chest expanded. It does not always come easy to sit with the torso perfectly aligned.
2) You may choose to keep your legs down or alternatively have leg, or both folded onto the seat of the chair.
3) With shoulders open and elbows up to chest level, assume a prayer stance with your palms together at the base of your sternum. Hold the position for 1 minute. Yes, it will be challenging at first to maintain this position for a full 60 seconds.
4) Inhale and exhale intentionally and keep moving your attention to the pelvis to make sure there is proper weight distribution and then to the upper body periodically.

This stance, like the mountain pose, enables you to look within and harmonize your physical and emotional selves. If you feel unstable performing the Easy Pose on a chair, you can sit on the floor if your mobility permits.

The Crescent Moon Bend (Urdhva Hastasana) #30

Side bends particularly help build flexibility in the ribcage and provide elasticity to the waist. An ache in the intercostal muscles (muscles located within the rib cage) is a common occurrence as we age and can be prevented by providing flexibility. When we bend sideways we are also activating a new movement for the spinal cord as it arches to a C-shape.

In traditional yoga asana, side-bends are believed to improve memory and concentration too.

How-to:

Scan For Audio

1) Keep the feet together and avoid moving them away from each other. Inhale and raise your arms and clasp the palms together above the crown and keep the stretched all through.
2) Exhale and bend to the right to form a crescent pose. Avoid any jerks and stop if you feel any discomfort. Keep the shoulders spread and away from the ears. Hold the position to observe the sensations of the body.
3) Inhale and get back to position. Bring hands back to the knees and relax. Repeat on the left side.

Take care to see that the waist, back, and neck are bending at the same time. It is a common error we observe when the neck gets tilted independent of the movement of the spine and is to be avoided.

Staff Pose (Dandasana) #31

It is a complete core-strengthening pose and you can start with one leg before you do both simultaneously.

How-to:

Scan For Audio

1) Sit in an upright position and this time push yourself deep into the chair to rest your back for support.
2) With your hands resting on the sides, lift up either one leg or both legs straight in front. Bring it parallel to the ground and if that seems too much, then as high as your hamstrings allow you. Pull the toes towards you.
3) Inhale and lift both arms up and hold the position for 5 counts. The spine should be stretched, the navel tucked in and the shoulders down.
4) Exhale and get back to position.

Shoulder Stretch With Strap #32

A yoga strap is useful to help us achieve difficult poses by providing alignment. You will find the range of motion increases dramatically when a strap is used.

How-to:

Scan For Audio

1) In the upright position, take hold of the strap with both hands ensuring the length of strap between your right and left hand is approximately a foot greater than your shoulder width.
2) Inhale and lift both hands up and stretch them over your head as much as possible. It will be possible to bring down the strap to the waist level and you will find the hands moving further back than it would without a band. Exhale and bring back the hands to knee level. Repeat at least five times. It will help reset your shoulder muscles and prompt them to move smoothly.
3) Inhale and lift the strap up to be held above the crown and bend to the right with the strap stretched and repeat on the left side. We must bear in mind to keep the movements slow and deliberate.

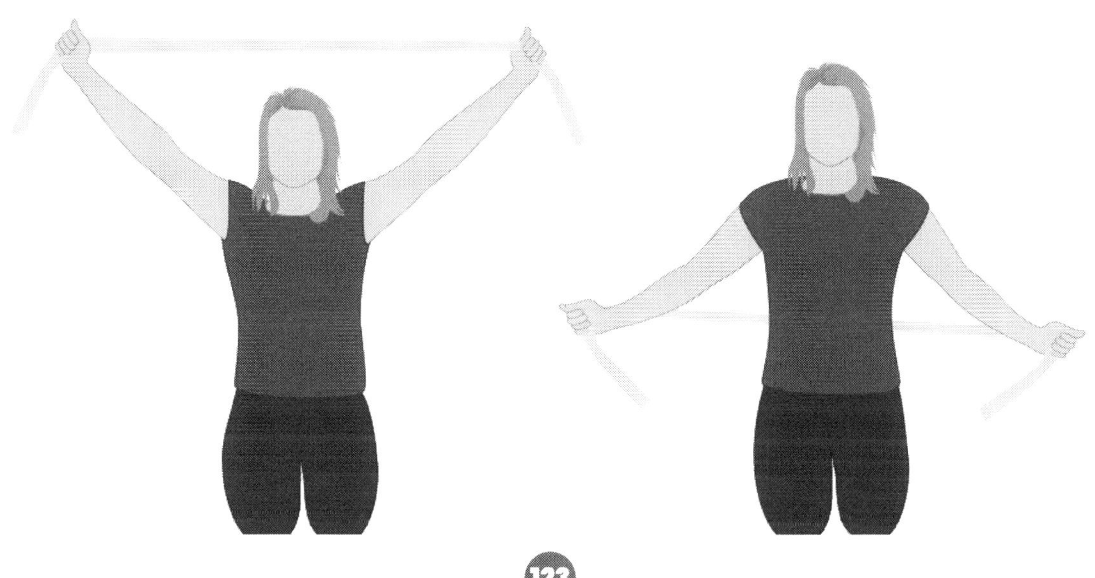

Hip Health

Hips surely get sensitive as we age. It does not fail to give signals when we shift on the couch or have to stand up after enjoying a television show. Keeping them happy is pertinent to our peace of mind.

The hip joint has a group of muscles that need to stay strong to support our body weight. Injuries are commonly caused when the hip joint loses flexibility and any minor stress causes them to dislocate. Get them used to a range of gentle motions every day and you will prevent harm to a large extent. But if you have pre-existing hip health issues, any exercise without consulting a medical expert is not advised.

Upper Body Twist Pose (Vakrasana) #33

How-to:

Scan For Audio

1) Sit upright with hands on the knees. Stretch your back as much as comfortable by pulling your shoulder blades together.
2) Inhale and turn the upper body to the right and look to the right, gazing as far as the eyes can see. Gently turn the neck but do not force the movement. Stay where you feel comfortable and remember that stiffness goes away only with long-term practice.
3) Exhale and come back to the mountain pose. Repeat on the left side.

It is a simple restorative pose that enhances the mobility of the vertebrae and tones abdominal muscles. It is great for aiding digestion as well.

Forward Bend (Upavistha Konasana) #34

How-to:

Scan For Audio

1) Sit in an upright position with your hands resting on the knees and gently spread both legs to the sides of the chair. The thighs will get into a V shape. Bend the knees to keep the heels and toes firmly on the ground. Sit tall with the spine straight and the head gently upwards.
2) Inhale and raise both your hands up by the sides of the ears. Hold for 2 seconds.
3) Exhale long and bend forward to have the upper body as parallel to the ground as possible. The hands would stay stretched with fingers pointing forward. Hold for 2 seconds.
4) If bending with your hands up in the air seems difficult, feel free to hold the chair on the sides or place them on your knees. As your flexibility increases you may wish to put blocks on the floor and stretch down to rest your palms on them. Yoga is all about gaining flexibility by not forcing the body.
5) Inhale and bring the upper body back to an upright position. Exhale and lower your hands by your sides. Keep the legs in the V shape keeping them on the sides of the chair.
6) Inhale and repeat from step (2).

This pose serves to prepare the hips for other postures and relaxes the spine. Use this pose as a warm-up when planning to engage the upper body with advanced postures.

Backward Bend #35

How-to:

Scan For Audio

1) Sit upright and follow step (1) of the Forward Bend pose. With your legs comfortably spread, hold the backrest of the chair at the hip level by taking your arms back. Inhale and bend your neck backward to look at the ceiling or sky.
2) Exhale and get back to the upright position. Be gentle and do not force the stretches. We need to always remember that the ideal pose is not the objective, the journey to achieving it is.

Side Angle Bend (Utthita Parsvakonasana) #36

This is a posture of medium difficulty level and should be attempted with caution if you have lower back issues.

How-to:

Scan For Audio

1) Follow step (1) of the Forward Bend pose. Gently bend to the left and try to reach your fingertips to the floor by sliding your hand down your left leg and ankle. If you cannot bend the full-length grasp the leg at the point where you stop. Placing a block or two on the sides of the legs will also help you support the bend.
2) As you bend to the left, straighten up the right arm and bring it to the left from over your head. Gaze up at the fingertips and stabilize the posture. Inhale and exhale a couple of times and get back to position. Repeat on the right side.

Chair Pose (Utkatasana) #37

This is a posture usually done standing and aiming to either sit on an imaginary chair or alternatively not quite sitting on a chair placed behind you. It is a simple-looking yet powerful pose that works on the glutes and diaphragm. It engages the pelvis and helps in centering your strength at the core. Progress very slowly with the repetitions as you need to build stamina. We will describe the progression from chair to an imaginary chair as our goal.

How-to:

Scan For Audio

1) Take the mountain posture (yes! with the care, the mindfulness, and the works) with your glutes on the forward end of the seat. Inhale and raise your hands to reach an almost vertical position but not quite there. The biceps will be by the side of your cheeks and not the ears and hold the position.
2) Exhale and lift yourself from the seat but not enough to reach a standing position. This may sometimes need you to bring your knees pressed against each other and your feet close to each other. The feet can be brought a little apart with some practice. The thigh muscles will engage and you will notice the lower back stretching downwards.
3) Keep the tailbone pushed downward and stay as if sitting on a higher chair. Stay for about ten seconds with your gaze directed to your toes. Inhale and get back to your real chair. Increase the number of repetitions gradually as your stamina improves.

Half Supine Pose (Ardha Supta Virasana) #38

How-to:

Scan For Audio

1) Sit in an upright position and hold the sides of the chair with both hands. Inhale, bend your right leg to bring the heel towards the back of the chair. You can use your right hand to help lift the leg.
2) Bring the heel to rest on the chair seat by the side if you can or continue to hold it. Hold and exhale.
3) Keep the spine straight at all times. Gently release the leg and bring it back to the ground. Repeat on the left side.

This pose helps in relaxing the thighs and improves the flexibility of the hips hence a must-try.

Sun Salutations (Suryanamaskar) #39

The sun is looked upon by all cultures as the ultimate source of energy and thus life. The sun salutation is a revered *yoga asana* done for holistic health. The graceful sequencing of multiple postures makes it a complete one to maintain body-mind balance, help in proper blood circulation, and stimulate multiple muscle groups, nerves, and internal organs apart from providing grace and tone to the body. This posture sequence has to be done without any hurry. Take time to hold to six counts with each posture shift.

How-to:

Scan For Audio

1) In the upright position bring your palms together in front of the chest in a prayer pose. Keep the feet at hip width at all times to maintain weight distribution. Keeping them close together will put you at risk of losing balance. Take a deep breath in and exhale slowly.
2) Inhale while lifting both hands to arch your body back. Hold while facing the sky and arms pushed back. Take care to see that you don't push more than the neck comfortably allows you to.
3) Exhale while bending down to bring the hands to the ground. The fingertips should touch the toes and not spread apart. It is fine if you cannot go the full length. Stretch and glance forward.
4) Inhale and lift the right leg towards the chest by clasping the hamstring with both palms. Rest the foot on the chair in case you find it tough to balance, lift the neck up to look to the ceiling, and hold for a few counts.
5) Holding this position slowly, bend your neck to rest the forehead on your knee by bringing the thighs further in, hold and release the leg back.
6) Exhale and bend again to similarly lift the left leg up. Hold, inhale and release to place the left foot back in position.

7) Exhale and bend forward to keep your palms on the shins. Continuing to bend, reach for the sides of the chair and give the spinal cord a gentle stretch forward while keeping the face looking forward.
8) Inhale and get back to the upright position with hands stretched up. Exhale and relax in the mountain posture.

Gate Pose (Parighasana) #40

How-to:

Scan For Audio

1) Take the upright position and turn the right leg to the right side of the chair to extend it fully. You will have the big toe touching the ground and the rest of the sole lifted. It will help you open up the hip joints.
2) Let your arms free on the side while you extend the leg and check your upper body alignment.
3) Take a breath in and raise your left arm to point straight up towards the sky. Allow the right arm to slip over the right leg.
4) Exhale and get back to an upright position. Repeat on the left side.
5) Once comfortable with the pose progress to elevating your left arm in an arch over your head, bending it to the right.

Chair Downward Dog (Adho Mukha Svanasana) #41

How-to:

Scan For Audio

1) Stand tall in front of your chair about one foot away while facing it. It is a good idea to keep the chair against a wall to prevent pushing it back. Keep your feet slightly apart and bend to place your palms on the chair seat. Once you feel stable walk your feet back about two strides each and keep the soles firmly on the ground. You will notice the spine stretch as you do this.
2) Hold on while firming up the biceps and shoulders. Engage the core and tuck the stomach in. The tailbone has to be stretched outward to release the tension. Inhale and exhale a few times in this position. Stand back gently and relax.
3) This pose provides relief to the spinal cord and stimulates blood circulation in the body. We can add variations by starting behind the chair to rest the forearms on the backrest instead of the seat to suit the flexibility of the body.
4) The downward dog doesn't have to be picture-perfect. In case you have difficulty bending because of an extra tight hip it is okay to kneel a little to bend the legs. Nobody is going to bite!

Modification

CHAPTER 11

Standing Postures

Instead of breaking when life presents difficulties, we bend with yoga.

Standing poses will help build your confidence in body balance. Go ahead and try postures with the chair by your side. We loved it the other day when Joey answered ' Well, we need chair yoga to bend so that we don't break.' We had just about begun a session with a group of new seniors and had a heart-to-heart on the introduction day.

As we age there is sometimes a tendency to walk with our legs apart to keep balance and feel secure. This can be corrected with postures that provide stability to the pelvis and hips and help the feet remain under the hips and not away.

The Right Chair for Standing Postures

The chair must have a backrest that is at the level of your diaphragm. Having a lower backrest will force you to bend forward while holding it and that is a complete no-no. We need the spine to be straight when you are standing. When you hold the backrest top with extended arms you will want to have them running parallel to the ground.

Sit to Stand Posture #42

This exercise will help people with serious mobility issues to strengthen the quadriceps or thigh muscles.

How-to:

Scan For Audio

1) Sit in an upright position, keep the legs slightly apart and cross your arms across the chest. Lean your body forward, inhale and use your legs to raise your buttocks to stand up straight.
2) Exhale deeply and sit back in an upright position. Repeat in slow and deliberate movements at least 8 times.

Tip: if initially you find it too difficult with your arms held across the chest try extending your arm at shoulder height and parallel to the floor.

Foot Raises #43

How-to:

Scan For Audio

1) Raise up from the chair and walk behind it. Stand in an upright position with the chair in front of you. Grab the backrest on the top and walk back to keep your arms extended without bending the elbow. Keep the feet close to and parallel to each other.
2) Inhale deeply and gently raise the heels with the body weight shifting to the metatarsals and toes. Hold four counts, exhale and get back to the heels. A common mistake here is that we tend to bend the ankles to the sides. Observe the ankle movements closely and it is moving up and down. We will run the risk of twisting the ankle if it moves sideways. Repeat a few times.
3) Inhale and this time raise the metatarsals and toes with the body weight on the heels. Hold, exhale and get back to the standing position. Repeat a few counts taking care not to exert the ankles. Relax by shaking out the legs. Bring your attention to the entire body as you move to make sure the back, shoulders, and neck are not slouching.

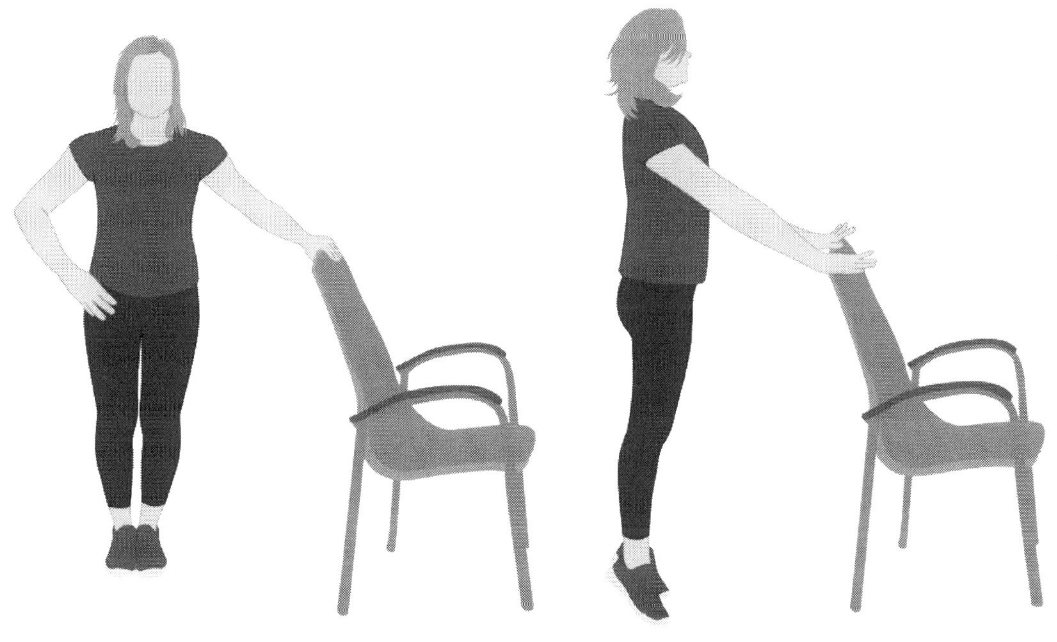

High Plank #44

How-to:

Scan For Audio

1) Raise from the chair and turn around to face it. Walk backward two steps to be able to bend and rest your palms on the backrest, you can progress to placing your palms on the seat of the chair. The chair must be sturdy enough to not slip, or consider placing it against a wall to ensure it cannot move backwards.
2) Keep the spine straight and bring the right foot to the front and bend at the knees. It should be at 90 degrees to the floor. Stretch the left leg back to keep it straight. Rest it on the toes by raising the heel.
3) The body weight would have now shifted to the hands. Gently take the right foot backwards and let it rest on the toes with the heel up. You will now have both the feet parallel.
4) The posture will make you feel like you are pushing the chair firmly into the ground. Take care to not allow the spine or elbows to bend or shoulders to droop while maintaining the posture. The high plank will help engage the core and build strength of the upper body and thighs.
5) Get back to an upright position with care and repeat with the left leg forward.

Modification

Standing Crane Pose #45

How-to:

Scan For Audio

1) Stand upright by the right side of your chair with feet close to each other. Hold the backrest with the left hand and stretch out the right hand on the side at chest level. Keep the palm facing downward and fingers pointing out.
2) Slowly slide the right foot up the inner ankle of the left foot with toes pointing forward and gradually bending the knee. Stop at the calf level with the knees bent well.
3) Adjust the posture of the entire body and hold for about five counts. You should be able to balance your body on one foot without wobbling. Stabilize to avoid the hips swaying to any particular side.
4) If you feel confident enough, gently lift the left hand from the backrest and stretch to the side to resemble a crane on one leg with wings spread. Hold for another five counts and move to the right side to repeat on the opposite side.

Practice regularly if you have balancing challenges and notice the change.

The Standing Tree Pose #46

This posture is a level more advanced than the crane pose and allows us to check and improve the balance in the body without too much support.

How-to:

Scan For Audio

1) Gently stand and move to the left side of the chair. Stand where you can comfortably hold the backrest for support. Hold the backrest with the right hand and swing the left hand to the side at chest level or slightly higher.
2) Lift your left foot and rest it on your lower calf muscle. Let go of the chair and spread the right hand as well to the side. You will feel the wobble on the right foot. Balance the body in this position for a few seconds. Use the chair backrest for support whenever needed.
3) As you gain stability, move the position of the left foot gradually up first to the shin, then the knee joint, to the inner thigh and finally near the top of the thigh. No matter whether your foot is raised to calf, shin, knee or upper thigh keep the sole of your foot firmly pressed to your leg to help maintain balance.
4) It will be a fantastic progression when you can balance the body with both hands spread out. The chair by your side is always an assurance. Use it to place your hands or just to touch with your fingertips in your expedition towards regaining full balance on one leg.
5) Celebrate the success and move to the right side of the chair to repeat.

Modification

Hip Extension #47

How-to:

Scan For Audio

1) Stand upright behind the chair and grasp the backrest by placing your palms on top of the chair.
2) Keep your feet together and slightly bend the knees. Gently raise the right foot and bring it behind you.
3) Push back the foot as much as possible and this extends the hips backward to activate the gluteus maximus, it being the main extensor muscle of the hip. Hold for a second, then return to the starting position. Since you are balancing on one foot during this drill, keep the weight on the arms to avoid wobbling.
4) To relax, lift up the right leg and swing it lightly to the right without bending the knee. Bring it back to position and repeat five times. With each swing try to get the leg higher. This will engage the hip muscles.
5) Switch legs are repeat the exercise with your left leg.

Forward Bend Hip Extension #48

How-to:

Scan For Audio

1) Stand tall behind the chair and grasp the top of the backrest. Inhale and walk back to get the arms straightened out. Exhale and bend forward to get the spine close to parallel to the ground. The arching of your back will reduce with practice.
2) Inhale and stretch the right leg forward with the toes facing up to rest on the heel. This action will extend the hip muscle for you.
3) Hold to feel the pull of the spine and the glute muscles. Exhale and get back to a standing position. Bend forward and repeat on the left side.

Chair Lunge #49

How-to:

Scan For Audio

1) Stand behind the chair, and hold the backrest with the arms extended. Gently bring the right leg back to extend it behind you as much as it allows you to.
2) Move the left leg forward. Take care to keep the left knee over the ankle during movement, moving further forward can cause knee problems. Tip: Placing the foot under the chair helps to ensure this as the chair will get in the way of the knee while moving further forward. Hold for a few moments to check your posture.
3) Bring the left foot back to position and then the right foot. Repeat with the right foot forward. This helps in regaining your balance and relaxing the pelvic floor muscles.
4) As your flexibility and confidence grows, bend your legs lower towards the floor.
5) You can also try the lunges with one hand up in the air. Raise the left hand when the right foot goes forward and vice versa.
6) The next progression will be to raise both hands. This will be a giant step forward. Don't worry! The chair is right next to you.

Modification (Low Lunge)

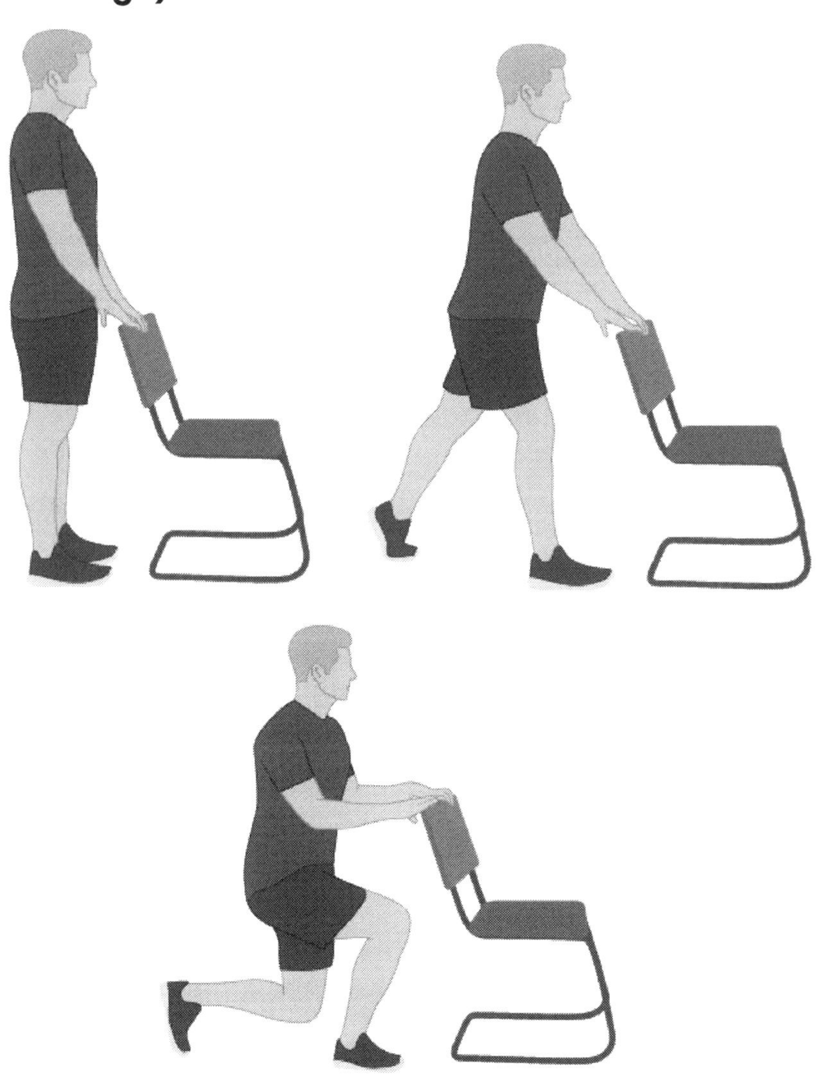

Standing Downward Dog #50

How-to:

Scan For Audio

1) Stand behind the chair and hold the top of the backrest. Walk back until the arms are fully extended and parallel to the ground.
2) Bend at the waist until your back is parallel to the ground. Keep the posture with the neck in between the biceps and face downwards.
3) Keep the pelvis muscles taut and feel the stretch of the arms, the spine, and the hamstrings. It is the goto posture that takes away stiffness from the whole body.
4) Progression is placing your palms on the chair seat

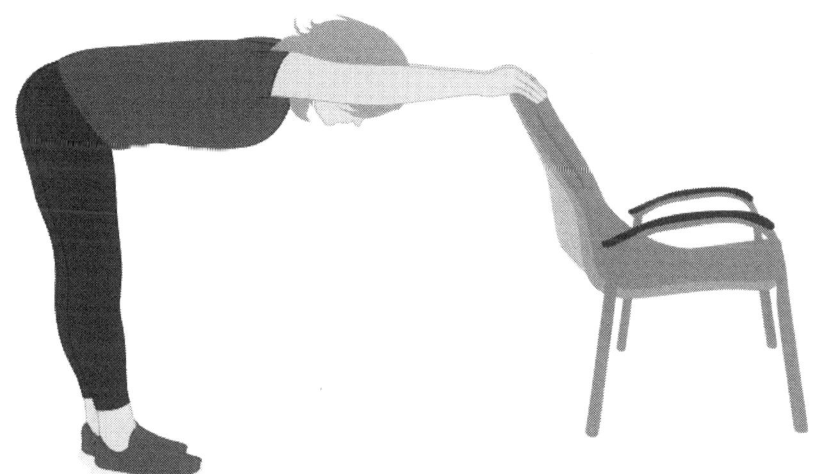

Modification

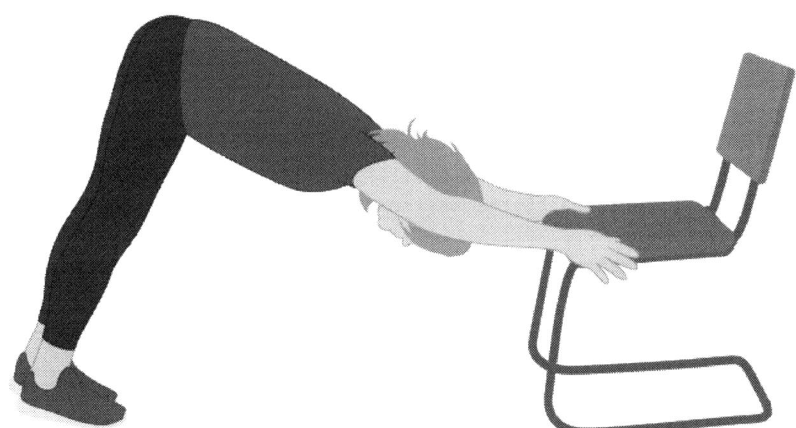

Side Arches #51

How-to:

Scan For Audio

1) Stand behind the chair with your body facing the side so that the left hand can hold the chair.
2) Inhale and raise your right arm keeping it stretched, and bring it over the head and bend to the left into a side bend. Here it is extremely important to keep the hip straight. Hold, exhale long and get back to position. If you imagine the pelvis to be a basket, it should remain straight and not tilt to the right. Move to the left corner of the chair and repeat on the opposite side.

Tight Rope #52

How-to:

Scan For Audio

It is a beautiful pose to help regain and improve balance.

1) Stand by the side or behind the chair. Place the left foot right behind the right foot as if you are standing on a rope. Inhale and spread your hands sideward like the wings of a bird and tummy tucked in.
2) Exhale and bring the hands back to the backrest. Repeat with the right foot behind this time. It seems simple but is a challenging one when you are working on building balance.
3) If you balance and confidence permit, try taking a few steps placing one foot just in front of the other, image yourself as a tight rope walker.

CHAPTER 12

Unwinding and Sleep Enhancing Chair Yoga Postures

A good laugh and a long sleep are the two best cures for anything.

—An Irish Proverb

We have our times when we are tired but end up tossing and turning without being able to slip into a good sleep. There are some wonderful restorative yoga postures that can help us to unwind and get quality sleep. You will need to sit in a quiet place and approach the exercises with an attitude of gaining a restful state. Spending around 15 minutes every day on these postures before sleep time will gradually help in getting us physically and psychologically prepared for good quality sleep. It's a good idea to string together the poses listed below with relaxing postures, such as the Child's pose and the Easy pose for constructive rest.

Forward Bending Pose (Uttanasana) #53

How-to:

Scan For Audio

1) Sit in the upright position with the legs kept at hip wide distance. You can use blocks under the feet or for you hands to rest on if you are feeling a strain in the spinal cord.
2) Inhale deeply while raising your hands straight above the crown. Sit tall to feel the rib cage expanding.
3) Exhale and bend from the waist to rest the upper body on your lap face downward and place your hands underneath the thighs. You can place a pillow on the lap to help you prolong the posture.
4) Hold the position for a minute and get back to an upright position. When done before bedtime it induces restful sleep.

Meditative Postures

Stay on the chair in an upright position with your hands resting on your knees. Close your eyes and follow your breathing as you inhale and exhale. Your mind will waver and will be occupied with thoughts or a sound may distract you. Do not resist but bring your attention back to the breath. Stay in this position for as long as you can. If you can sustain for let's say thirty seconds you have done an excellent job for a beginner. In case you find it uncomfortable, you will be relieved to know that you are not alone. In our experience, way too many people have reported nervousness, anxiety, or good old fear when they try closing their eyes and staying still.

Do not resist any thought that comes to your mind. Observe it and let it pass. Do the same with the next thought. You will gradually find yourself detaching from your thoughts and observing them like an onlooker. This is a powerful position to attain. The next time you find yourself becoming impulsive in either positive or negative emotions, you will not lose control. Developing this state of composure is great for your mental well-being. The Vedas speak in great detail of how positive and negative emotions are to be dealt with, with equanimity and dualities sought to be diminished. Practicing simple meditation with a focus on breathing brings about mental equilibrium and trains it to be less fickle and less impulsive.

Hands Over Heart (Sukhasana) #54

How-to:

Scan For Audio

1) It is a variation of the Easy Pose and is designed to bring stability and calm. Sit upright and bring your hands to the chest with palms overlapping.
2) Keep your eyes closed or alternatively have a soft gaze downwards. Take deep breaths and get into the feeling of loving kindness for yourself. Keep the exhalations longer to induce a restful state.
3) Another effective variation is to keep one hand on the heart while the other rests on the belly to help you feel the breathing more intensely to prevent the mind from wandering.

Dead Person or Corpse Pose (Savasana) #55

The name indicates that we take the posture of a dead person to depict a deep state of complete relaxation and surrender. It symbolizes absence of tension in the muscles and mind. This pose is an important one in all the traditional schools of *yogasana*. It can soothe the entire nervous system and remove fatigue.

Savasana is interestingly an easy read but challenging to master. If distraction were a person they would jump with glee when someone decided to do this one! This is because once the body gets into the state of inertia there is a strong tendency to doze off or for the mind to get busy with thoughts. The dead man pose is a posture for rest but not sleep and the mind has to be in the present with no thoughts. Hmm...

How-to:

Scan For Audio

1) Slip your glutes to the forward edge of the seat and spread your shoulders wide to lay them flat on the backrest of your chair. Allow your head to rest on the rim of the chair. You could place a folded towel on the headrest if the surface is hard and a pillow or bolster behind you on the seat before you start. Take your time to adjust to the most comfortable position.
2) Once your head rests on the chair, pay attention to the legs, push them forward and stretch as much as possible without the head not slipping down. Rest the sole on the floor.
3) Let the arms hang free by the sides of the chair like you see a corpse in movies.
4) Keep your eyes closed and breathe easy(of course!) and let the tongue rest on the floor of the mouth. Be in a complete state of relaxation and yielding. Stay in this state of rest for anywhere from 5 to 20 minutes.
5) Once done, open your eyes slowly and get into an upright position without any sudden movements.

A word of caution: Since this pose can lead you to fall asleep, one needs to be aware of possible falls from the chair. It will be safe to have someone around to alert you or maybe set an alarm to get you. Relaxing with attention is a tall order!

If your mobility allows this pose can also be performed on the floor, which removes the possibility of falling from the chair if you doze off.

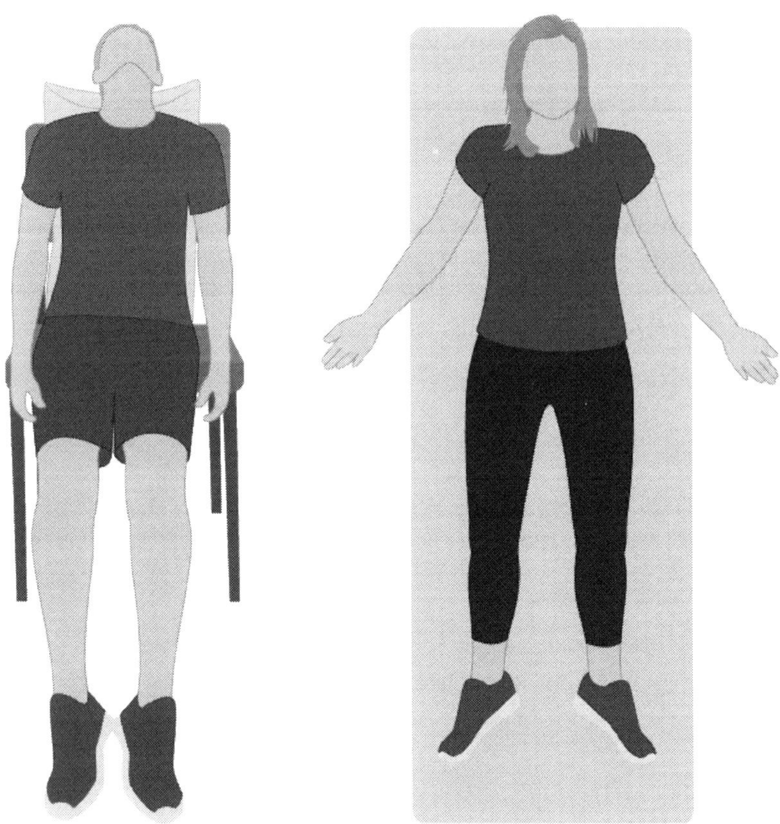

CHAPTER 13

Postures for Further Progress

It is not whether you get knocked down; it's whether you get up.

—Vince Lombardi

Once you have had a go at the beginner's postures and noticed the benefits, you would want to try out the more advanced postures. Try out new postures to gain more but take care to follow your body and respect its limits. Accept that it is where it is. Offer no physical or mental resistance to the situation. You will find the body becoming more malleable over time. Deep breathing is to be practiced in a completely relaxed manner at all times. It is not okay to feel dizzy or stressed at any point in time. The mantra is to progress gradually.

Fire Log Pose (Agnistambhasana) #56

This is a difficult pose as it requires you to cross both legs on the seat of the chair and hence attempt only if you feel up to it. If you are able, I suggest performing the Fire Log pose sitting on the floor. Although it is then not a chair yoga exercise, you may find it easier to achieve.

How-to:

Scan For Audio

1) Sit upright, inhale and lift the right leg, bend the knee and place the right foot on the left thigh. Exhale, and hold for a few seconds to feel the sensations. You will feel the hamstrings pull and the ankles twist.
2) Inhale. Bend the left leg and place the left foot under the right knee. The legs will resemble fire logs placed on top of each other.
3) Exhale and hold a few moments with your spine erect, chin up and eyes gazing ahead.
4) Disengage by slowly releasing the legs one at a time and reestablishing the mountain pose. Take deep deliberate breaths and relax.

If your hip flexibility doesn't allow the right leg to lay flat, place a rolled up towel to support the leg.

If your mobility permits, you may prefer to perform this pose sitting on the floor, 3 variants are illustrated below.

Floor versions

Knee Hugs (Apanasana) #57

This pose will challenge you a bit but do not worry about getting it perfect in the initial days. You would by now know that each part of your body has a mind of its own and will take a bit of coaxing to comply.

The knee hug engages the whole body. It is also good for the stomach helping relieve constipation and bloating and rejigs the digestive juices. If your days are otherwise sedentary this asana will rejuvenate you for sure.

How-to:

Scan For Audio

1) Raise the right leg parallel to the floor with the left leg firmly rooted.
2) Hold on to the right thigh and gently raise it, bend the knees, inhale and draw in the leg towards your chest as if in a hug.
3) Backbone loosen up and it is a wonderful feeling. Exhale and straighten back the leg. Place it back on the floor and repeat with the left leg.
4) Once you get a hang of it with one leg at a time, gently place both legs one at a time on the edge of the chair to achieve a two-knee-to-chest hug. Hold on to the sides of the chair to keep balance and once both legs are stable on the chair across the arms give your legs a warm hug.
5) Inhale and exhale with your spine kept straight. You will feel the upper arm stretching and the stomach muscles straining a little. Be aware of the sensations and remain in complete acceptance of the body.

If your mobility allows you can perform this pose lying on the floor, which some may actually find easier.

Floor versions

The Seated Camel Pose (Ustrasana) #58

How-to:

Scan For Audio

1) Sit toward the front of the chair and place hands on either the side of the chair seat or hold the sides of the backrest.
2) Now slowly bend arch your back
3) You may find it easier with yoga blocks placed under your feet

The Kneeling Camel Pose #58A

How-to:

Scan For Audio

4) It will be helpful to have a wall behind the chair to prevent it from accidentally slipping backward.
5) Sit upright with knees clasped together. Place your palms on the sides of the seat and breathe in. As you exhale slowly move forward, bend your knees, and slip out of the chair to eventually kneel on the ground.
6) Now place your palms on hips and bend backward. Release your hands place them on the chair seat or its backrest. Hold on for a while and get back to the kneeling position with the back straight and palms on the hips.
7) Inhale, exhale, and rejoice in the momentary freedom from the chair. Now that you are done, allow your hands to reach the support of the seat of the chair. Once you have got hold, prop yourself up and get back to the safety of the chair. Here is where you need a wall behind the chair to prevent any slip whilst getting back.
8) The camel posture tones up the spine and we bet you will look forward to more reps.

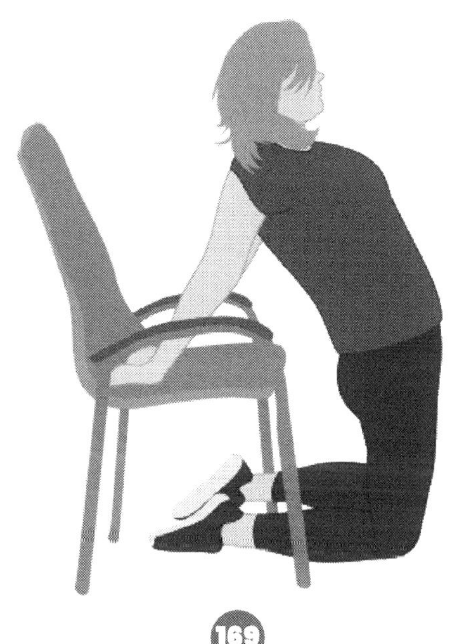

Forward Bend With Wide Leg Pose (Prasarita Padottanasana) #59

How-to:

Scan For Audio

1) Sit upright in the mountain pose and bring the buttocks forward towards the front edge.
2) Spread the legs sideways so that the knees move to the seat edge with the toes going outwards.
3) Place your palms on the hips and look upwards. Slowly release the hands and extend them together towards the ground while bending forwards.
4) The face should be facing forwards and not downwards. Continue bending while tucking the tummy in as far forward as you comfortably can, The ultimate goal is to bend until your palms rest flat on the ground. You will naturally be exhaling while bending. Pay attention to your breathing.
5) Hold this position for a while. If you are fine with this posture, you will proceed to look down and try to bend your head toward the ground. Stop when you feel out of balance to prevent a risk of falling.

Kneeling Elbow Shoulder Stretch #60

This is a posture of medium difficulty level and an efficient way to tone up the biceps and shoulders.

How-to:

Scan For Audio

1) Stand facing the chair. Kneel and bend forward placing both elbows on the chair seat with the spine parallel to the floor. Rest the crown of the head on the edge of the chair facing downwards. Stabilize and hold for a few counts.
2) Turn the palms towards you and bring them towards the shoulder blades as far as they can go. This will get the posterior muscles of the arms to tone up.

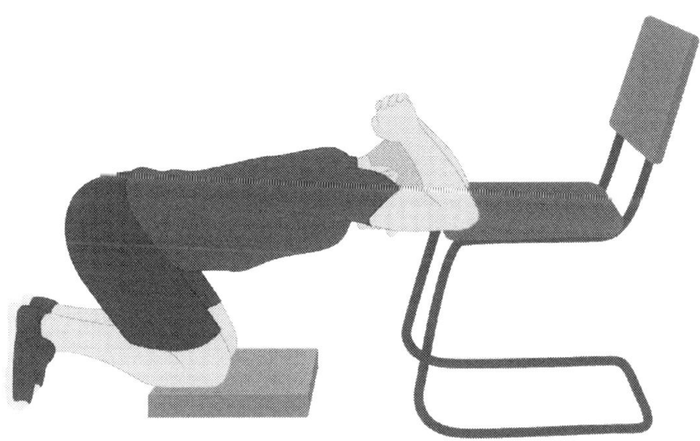

The Extended Triangle (Utthita Trikonasana) #61

Is a posture requiring a certain amount of ability to bend and stretch on the chair. It is advisable to proceed to this only after you have achieved suppleness in movements with the beginner poses.

How-to:

Scan For Audio

1) Sit in the mountain pose and bring yourself a little forward to the edge of the chair. Raise your arms sideways parallel to the floor and spread them straight like a bird about to take off.
2) Now get your legs to spread like a triangle with the soles going as far sideways and outwards as comfortable.
3) Once you find yourself stable, exhale and bend sideways to the right to get your right hand to touch the floor (or as far down your leg towards the floor as is possible) with your fingertips. Both arms should maintain a straight line position.
4) Being able to touch the floor could be an ambitious thought for a starter but is easily achievable with some practice. Turn your gaze up and keep them locked to your left arm. Remain in this position for as long as you can hold it while breathing evenly.
5) Get back to the vertical position with hands and legs spread and repeat to the left side. Keep the movements slow and with no jerks or force. Your attention should be constantly brought back to the body parts that are being used to achieve the posture. Feel the shoulder muscles loosen up and the hamstring crackle up in joy.

Progression here is to perform the Triangle standing and placing the palm of one hand on the chair seat.

It will help remove stiffness of the lower back and provides relief to lifestyle-induced backaches along with providing suppleness to the hips, arms, and legs. Blood flow to the lower body increases due to increased movement. Regular practice will help remove the accumulation of fat around the midriff. You can also practice the Triangle pose standing resting your hand on the chair seat.

The Warrior Pose 3 (Virabhadrasana 3) #62

How-to:

Scan For Audio

1) Stand behind the chair and place both hands on the backrest. Step back from the chair. You may wish to place the chair against a wall to ensure it does not move as you perform the pose. Keeping your arm straight slowly bend forward from the waist. Breathe in and out a few times.
2) Slowly take the left leg off the ground. This will not be difficult as it will be a natural counter-balance the tilting of the body forward. Hold on for about 10 seconds in balance.
3) Pay attention to your breathing and get back. Repeat on the left. Doing this consistently will find yourself building better balance in the body and mental agility.
4) As your balance improves progress by first stand further back from the chair and then to placing your hands on the chair seat.

Modification

Seated Forward Bend (Paschimottanasana) #63

The name is to indicate that the focus of discussion is the back of the body since traditionally yogis practiced their asanas facing the rising sun in the east. It stretches the entire range of muscles beginning with the Achilles tendon all the way to the crown.

You will need another chair in front to support your legs.

How-to:

Scan For Audio

1) Sit in an upright position with another chair placed in front of you at a distance where you can reach your shins to rest on.
2) Raise one leg at a time and place them on the chair and make sure the calf muscles are well supported.
3) Inhale and slowly lift both arms high, exhale and bend the upper body to rest your face on your lap. It will not be easy to achieve this initially, but any bend is a worthwhile posture.
4) Aim for your hands to reach as far down towards your feet as possible. Stop where you feel resistance and hold the legs. This will stretch the back all the way from the heel to the head and help you become more flexible.

Reverse Table Top Pose (Ardhapurvottanasana) #64

How-to:

Scan For Audio

1) Take a chair and position it in front of the wall with the backrest touching the wall. Turn your back to the chair and seat yourself on the ground about a foot way from the chair. Alternatively sit on the chair and then get yourself on to the floor using the chair as a support.
2) Push yourself back so that the seat touches your back. Inhale and bend your neck to gently rest your nape and head on the chair seat. Bend your arms back as well and rest your palms on the chair seat or alternatively hold the backrest. Hold for 4 counts, exhale and get back to sitting position.

It develops mobility of the upper back to release tension from the shoulder muscles. Avoid the posture if you have been diagnosed with cervical spondylitis.

CONCLUSION

When Yale University Professor Laurie Santos began a small session at her residence in the University for her stressed-out students she did not expect 'The Science of Well-Being', as the course came to be known, to become the most popular course in the 300-year-old history of Yale. It spread like wildfire with its online presence and peaking post-pandemic, and the university was left clamoring to manage its popularity. In essence, it speaks about how our brains have misconceptions about what makes us happy and what needs to be prioritized. In its list of priorities come savoring experiences, gratitude, and good sleep, and we can't help drawing parallels to what the yoga sutras say about the road to a meaningful life.

This book is dedicated to all the courageous souls who have decades of life experience, have endured wear and tear, successes, and sorrows, and are now seeking to live a more meaningful life. Knowing that there aren't many golden-agers who yearn to be younger is consoling. From chats, it seems that one would not exchange their tranquil old age for anything. You can be assured that practicing chair yoga will boost your creativity and resilience as you age. The younger generation needs to perceive an optimistic future version of themselves.

Demotivation is more often than not a natural by-product of attempting to begin something new. You will have ample, overt, and covert resistance within yourself, from others, and from the environment. Once we accept that there is always a price to pay for the change to set in, nothing should stop us. We will wage the gentle war to keep our dignity intact. Continue listening to, reading, and researching reliable sources for information because knowledge is dynamic and no one source has all the answers. The transformation you achieve will be contagious for sure.

Yoga through its philosophy talks loud and clear about interdependence, the idea that we are connected. It is fascinating to observe that the elements and characteristics of nature are referenced in the Sanskrit titles of the postures. You will find many of the postures named after birds, aquatic animals, mammals, vegetation, and even insects. Some of the asanas are named after incarnations, mythological characters, and revered sages that help us acknowledge the unity of creation and advance away from separatism.

Start your new routine with very gentle and elegant steps that will make you feel better right away and inspire your family and friends by demonstrating newfound energy. It will help to convince our community that chair yoga is for real people, unlike the idea we get from posture boys and girls in the media. Within days of spending time with chair yoga, you will notice a significant change in terms of achieving coordination of your body, the senses, and thoughts that in turn will bring harmony to your other actions as well. You will notice that you are walking, working, doing chores, and talking with more purpose and intent. Like Victor, you would have finally found your mojo.

Spread the Word

If you enjoyed this book as much as we have enjoyed writing it, and if you feel that the chair yoga instruction and poses that you've received here will positively improve your both your lifestyle and mental wellbeing, please tell others.

Spread the word by referrals to friends, family, and other seniors (and soon-to-be seniors) whom you know, and who you think can benefit.

Our Community:

To be one of the first people to receive notification of future books in the series "For Seniors 50, 60 and Beyond" when they are released join our community. I'll personally notify you as soon the next book in the series is available. Our monthly newsletter also contains tip, tricks and advice to help you on your fitness journey.

We Have A Favor To Ask:

Would you please take a couple of minutes to write a review of this book on Amazon? We'll be checking the reviews personally and your honest feedback will help us better help others starting out on their chair yoga journey.

To Leave A Review:

- Please can the QR code below

or

- Visit Amazon's website, search *Chair Yoga for Seniors 50, 60 and Beyond*. Click the link for this book, scroll down, and click on "Write a Customer Review."

  https://www.amazon.com/dp/B0C5W62JNC

Thank you so much, and we look forward to reading your comments!

David and Florence

For Seniors 50, 60 and Beyond

BOOK SERIES

Book 1: **Fitness For Seniors 50, 60 and Beyond**

It's never too early to improve your fitness and definitely never to late to start. Consider this a fitness guide book, dip into to its sections as and when required.

Book 2: **Resistance Bands For Seniors 50, 60 and Beyond**

Strength and flexibility training without the need to purchase expensive weights and with less risk of injury, or a gym membership.

Book 3: **Balance Exercise For Seniors 50, 60 and Beyond**

Improve your balance to significantly reduce the risk and overcome the fear of falling. Live an active life in your golden years with increased self-confidence.

Book 4: **Chair Yoga For Seniors 50, 60 and Beyond**

All the benefits of yoga achievable while sitting or using a chair for additional support. Chair yoga offers variations that are perfect for seniors, even for those with limited mobility.

Book 5: **Stretches For Seniors 50, 60 and Beyond**

Stretches to improve flexibility, balance, mobility and reduce muscle pain for beginner through to advanced practitioners. Stretching helps release muscle tension, soreness and reduces the risk of injury.

Book 6: **Core Training For Seniors 50, 60 and Beyond**

A strong core stabilizes your entire body, providing better balance and posture. Core strength is essential at any age but especially as you get older and your risk of falling increases.

An overview of the For Seniors 50, 60 and Beyond book series is available at www.iaa.pub or scan the QR code.

SCAN FOR BOOK INFORMATION

Glossary

Achilles Tendon: A tough band of fibrous tissue that connects the calf muscles to the heel bone.

Anabolic: The 'building up' aspect of metabolism to maintain the functioning of the body.

Catabolic: The 'breaking down' aspect of metabolism to maintain the functioning of the body.

Contraindication: A condition that makes the activity risky.

Cortisol: A hormone that has anti-inflammatory and immunosuppressive properties.

Dementia: A general term for impaired ability to remember, think or make decisions and interfere with everyday activities.

Dialysis: A clinical purification of blood as a substitute for the normal function of the kidney.

Diaphragm: A dome-shaped muscular partition separating the chest cavity from the abdomen.

Endorphins: A group of hormones secreted from the brain and nervous systems.

Insomnia: A common sleep disorder that makes it hard to fall or stay asleep.

Melatonin: A hormone the brain produces in response to darkness that helps in setting the sleep cycle.

Metatarsals: A group of long bones on the foot located behind the toes.

Multiple Sclerosis: A potentially disabling disease of the brain and spinal cord.

Neuroplasticity: Ability of the brain to form and reorganize synaptic connections in response to new learning.

Pelvic Floor: A group of muscles found in the base of your pelvis that houses the bladder, uterus/prostate, and rectum.

Psycho physiology: A study of the relationship between mind and body.

Restless Leg Syndrome: A condition that causes an uncontrollable urge to move the legs, usually because of an uncomfortable sensation.

Spondylitis: A condition in which the spine becomes inflamed.

Synovial fluid: A fluid with an egg-white-like consistency found in the cavities of joints.

Tennis Elbow: A condition that causes pain around the elbow because of overuse of muscles of the forearm.

Torso: The trunk of the human body without the head, arms, or legs.

References

Robinson, K. (2006). *Do schools kill creativity?* Ted.com; TED Talks. https://www.ted.com/talks/sir_ken_robinson_do_schools_kill_creativity?language=en

9 Yogic Breathing Practices for Mind-Body Balance and Healing. (n.d.). https://www.himalayanyogainstitute.com/9-yogic-breathing-practices-mind-body-balance-healing/

10 Min YOGA FOR ELBOW PAIN Relief – Tennis Elbow and Golfer's Elbow Stretches. (n.d.). Www.youtube.com. Retrieved October 12, 2022, from https://www.youtube.com/watch?v=r_0OR1cMA0s

10 Minute Chair Yoga for Joint Pain Relief. (n.d.). Www.youtube.com. Retrieved October 12, 2022, from https://www.youtube.com/watch?v=xYuLL21CIUw

Accessible Yoga Podcast. (n.d.). Www.accessibleyoga.org. Retrieved October 12, 2022, from https://www.accessibleyoga.org/podcasts/accessible-yoga-podcast

ademarsh. (2007, August 28). *Wide-Angled Seated Forward Bend*. Yoga Journal. https://www.yogajournal.com/poses/wide-angle-seated-forward-bend/

B K S Iyengar, & Yehudi Menuhin. (2014). *Light on yoga : yoga dipika*. Harper Collins.

Basavaraddi, I. (2015, April 23). *Yoga: Its Origin, History and Development*. Www.mea.gov.in. https://www.mea.gov.in/search-result.htm?25096/Yoga:_su_origen

Büssing, A., Michalsen, A., Khalsa, S. B. S., Telles, S., & Sherman, K. J. (2012, September 12). *Effects of Yoga on Mental and Physical Health: A Short Summary of Reviews*. Evidence-Based Complementary and Alternative Medicine. https://www.hindawi.com/journals/ecam/2012/165410/

Center for Health Care Strategies. (2018). *What is trauma-informed care?* Trauma-Informed Care Implementation Resource Center. https://www.traumainformedcare.chcs.org/what-is-trauma-informed-care/

Chair Yoga and Why Seated Yoga Poses Are Good For You. (n.d.). Lifespan. https://www.lifespan.org/lifespan-living/chair-yoga-and-why-seated-yoga-poses-are-good-you

Chair Yoga Sun Salutations. (n.d.). Www.youtube.com. Retrieved October 12, 2022, from https://www.youtube.com/watch?v=kpmxmkyyzCI

Collins, S. (n.d.). *Stretching: How to Stretch, When to Stretch*. WebMD. https://www.webmd.com/fitness-exercise/features/how-to-stretch

DiBenedetto, M., Innes, K. E., Taylor, A. G., Rodeheaver, P. F., Boxer, J. A., Wright, H. J., & Kerrigan, D. C. (2005). Effect of a Gentle Iyengar Yoga Program on Gait in the Elderly: An Exploratory Study. *Archives of Physical Medicine and Rehabilitation*, *86*(9), 1830–1837. https://doi.org/10.1016/j.apmr.2005.03.011

Domonell, K. (2016, June 13). *7 Things You're Doing Totally Wrong During Yoga Class*. Women's Health. https://www.womenshealthmag.com/fitness/g19976952/yoga-mistakes/

Foundation, W. S. (n.d.). *Yoga vs Exercise*. White Swan Foundation. Retrieved October 12, 2022, from https://www.whiteswanfoundation.org/mental-health-matters/wellbeing/yoga-vs-exercise#:~:text=Yoga%3A%20In%20yoga%2C%20the%20body

goldmanb@stanford.edu, img src='//sgec stanford edu/content/dam/sm-news/images/2019/11/goldman-bruce-90 jpg img 620 high png' alt='Bruce G. B. B. G. B. G. is a science writer in the O. of C. E. him at. (2017, March 30). *Study shows how slow breathing induces tranquility*. News Center. https://med.stanford.edu/news/all-news/2017/03/study-discovers-how-slow-breathing-induces-tranquility.html

Healthy Practices - Stuff that Really Makes Us Happy. (n.d.). Coursera. Retrieved October 12, 2022, from https://www.coursera.org/learn/the-science-of-well-being/lecture/X2Agx/healthy-practices

Hip Opening Poses. (n.d.). Yoga Basics. Retrieved October 12, 2022, from https://www.yogabasics.com/practice/pose-type/hip-opening-poses/

Hoffman, H. (2019, April 19). *Benefits of Yoga for Stroke Recovery*. Saebo. https://www.saebo.com/blog/benefits-of-yoga-for-stroke-recovery/#:~:text=New%20research%20suggests%20that%20adding

How Yoga Can Help People With Dementia. (n.d.). Yogainternational.com. https://yogainternational.com/article/view/how-yoga-can-help-people-with-dementia

How Yoga Can Improve Your Sleep Quality. (n.d.). Sleep Foundation. https://www.sleepfoundation.org/physical-activity/yoga-and-sleep

Ikai, S., Uchida, H., Mizuno, Y., Tani, H., Nagaoka, M., Tsunoda, K., Mimura, M., & Suzuki, T. (2017). Effects of chair yoga therapy on physical fitness in patients with psychiatric disorders:

A 12-week single-blind randomized controlled trial. *Journal of Psychiatric Research*, *94*, 194–201. https://doi.org/10.1016/j.jpsychires.2017.07.015

Know your workout well! 10 differences between yoga and exercise. (2022, March 28). Healthshots. https://www.healthshots.com/fitness/staying-fit/know-your-workout-well-10-differences-between-yoga-and-exercise/

Lawrence, M., Celestino Junior, F. T., Matozinho, H. H., Govan, L., Booth, J., & Beecher, J. (2017). Yoga for stroke rehabilitation. *Cochrane Database of Systematic Reviews*. https://doi.org/10.1002/14651858.cd011483.pub2

Liveyogalife.com | Chair pose yoga, Yoga for seniors, Chair yoga. (n.d.). Pinterest. Retrieved October 12, 2022, from https://in.pinterest.com/pin/197595502377184594/

Malik, S., Dua, R., Bhadoria, A., & Kumar, R. (2021). Chair Yoga. *Journal of Medical Evidence*, *2*(3), 262. https://doi.org/10.4103/jme.jme_5_21

Monson, N. (n.d.). *VA study finds 20 veterans die by suicide each day*. Retrieved November 14, 2022, from https://www.mentalhealthfirstaid.org/cs/wp-content/uploads/2016/11/USA-Today-Mental-Health-First-Aid.pdf

Paranjpe, A. (2021). What is Yoga Psychology and Where Does It Stand in Contemporary Psychology? *Psychology and Developing Societies*, *33*(2), 155–174. https://doi.org/10.1177/09713336211038809

Parker, C. B. (2014, September 5). *Stanford scholar helps veterans recover from war trauma*. Stanford University. https://news.stanford.edu/news/2014/september/meditation-helps-ptsd-090514.html#:~:text=A%20Stanford%20scholar%20has%20found

says, Y. S. (2017, January 20). *The Benefits of Yoga & Meditation For Alzheimers & Dementia*. The Minded Institute. https://themindedinstitute.com/clarity-within-haze-benefits-yoga-meditation-alzheimers-dementias/

Davidson, R. J. (n.d.). *How mindfulness changes the emotional life of our brains | Richard J. Davidson | TEDxSanFrancisco*. Www.ted.com. https://www.ted.com/talks/richard_j_davidson_how_mindfulness_changes_the_emotional_life_of_our_brains_jan_2019?language=en

Schmid, A. A., Miller, K. K., Van Puymbroeck, M., & DeBaun-Sprague, E. (2014). Yoga leads to multiple physical improvements after stroke, a pilot study. *Complementary Therapies in Medicine*, *22*(6), 994–1000. https://doi.org/10.1016/j.ctim.2014.09.005

Standing Chair Yoga for Posture, balance, 50+, senior women, anti aging, grace and health. (n.d.). Www.youtube.com. Retrieved October 12, 2022, from https://www.youtube.com/watch?v=u34924N7B-o&t=100s

TEDx Talks. (2015). Breathe to Heal | Max Strom | TEDxCapeMay. In *YouTube*. https://www.youtube.com/watch?v=4Lb5L-VEm34

Ten Reasons to Do Chair Yoga | Yoga Alliance. (n.d.). Www.yogaalliance.org. Retrieved October 12, 2022, from https://www.yogaalliance.org/About_Yoga/Article_Archive/Ten_Reasons_to_Do_Chair_Yoga

Ten yoga mudras and Their benefits. (n.d.). Dragonfly Yoga Studio. Retrieved October 12, 2022, from https://www.dragonfly-yoga.org/blog/ten-yoga-mudras-and-their-benefits-1#:~:text=Mudras%20are%20a%20set%20of

Thomas, C. M. (2021). *Sleep and Brain Injury*. Routledge.

What Every Yogi Needs to Know About Flexibility. (2021, March 30). Yoga Journal. https://www.yogajournal.com/practice/beginners/what-science-can-teach-us-about-flexibility/

What Is 4-7-8 Breathing? (n.d.). Verywell Mind. Retrieved October 12, 2022, from https://www.verywellmind.com/what-is-4-7-8-breathing-5204438#:~:text=Andrew%20Weil.

Yoga. (n.d.). Yoga.ayush.gov.in. https://yoga.ayush.gov.in/blog?q=58

Yoga For Hands, Fingers, Wrists | 11-Minute Yoga Quickie | Yoga With Adriene. (n.d.). Www.youtube.com. Retrieved October 12, 2022, from https://www.youtube.com/watch?v=NxC4LhOrMFw

Yoga Props 101: Blocks, Straps, Blankets, and Bolsters. (2018, July 19). Chopra. https://chopra.com/articles/yoga-props-101-blocks-straps-blankets-and-bolsters

Asana – Inkpots & Daydreams. Accessed 14 Nov. 2022. www.terriguillemets.com/20020510-1902-yoga-poses/.

Exercise Index

Made in United States
Troutdale, OR
12/02/2024

25695978R00106